EFFECTIVE BUSINESS SPEAKING

by Judith A. McManus

LearningExpress • New York

Library of Congress Cataloging-in-Publication Data

McManus, Judith A.
    Effective business speaking / Judith McManus.
        p.   cm.—(Basics made easy)
    ISBN 1–57685–146–X
    1. Business communication.   2. Oral communication.   3. Public speaking.   I. Title.
II. Series.
HF5718.M436   1998
658.4′5—dc21   98–26231
                                                                                              CIP

Printed in the United States of America
9 8 7 6 5 4 3 2
First Edition

For Further Information
For information on LearningExpress, other LearningExpress products, or bulk sales, please call or write to us at:
    LearningExpress®
    900 Broadway
    Suite 604
    New York, NY 10003

CONTENTS

CHAPTER 1

THE IMPORTANCE OF EFFECTIVE COMMUNICATION

Being able to communicate effectively is a highly valued skill in the workplace. Many surveys indicate that executives in business and government rank good communication as a top priority for their employees. Why? Because each day in businesses around the world, thousands of hours are spent on the creation and dissemination of oral messages. These messages are delivered in meetings, interviews, sales promotions, customer service relations, and formal presentations. Research indicates that you spend a minimum of 50% of your time at work communicating with others. If you're a manager, salesperson, or customer service representative, the average time you spend talking to other people jumps up to 80%.

It has also been estimated that millions of dollars are wasted each year due to poor communication skills. Recent surveys indicate that 70% of customers do not return to businesses at which the service is poor. In addition, research shows that a dissatisfied customer will tell approximately seven people about the problem. And then those people will tell others about the poor service. In many cases, customer dissatisfaction is caused by, or at least aggravated by, poor communication between customers and service providers. The bottom line is that poor communication can amount to a cascade of lost revenue for a company.

EFFECTIVE COMMUNICATION MEANS GOOD SERVICE

More than likely your company has many competitors that offer the same product or service for the same price. Effective communication and excellent service may be the deciding factor that distinguishes your business from another. An article in *Training/Human Resource* magazine cited a study that rated communication skills as the second most important skill in a businessperson's success.

Sunil Padiyar, an executive for SalesLogix, a multimillion-dollar computer company, aptly states, "In today's competitive world, effective public speaking is critical to the success of an individual and the company he or she represents." Another top executive, John Jacobs of Eller Media, points out, "Our employees must have good communication skills with a focus on organization, delivery, and service." The bottom line is that whatever your job and whatever your aspiration, you need to deliver your message in a clear and coherent manner.

CREDIBILITY AND CONFIDENCE

There is a major bonus for you when you can communicate effectively. People assume that if you can give a speech, communicate at a meeting, or handle that

 ## WORDS FROM THE WISE

"There's only one corner of the universe you can be certain of improving, and that's your own self. So you have to begin there, not outside, not on other people. That comes afterwards, when you have worked on your own corner."

—*Aldous Huxley*

"To develop ease and confidence in doing, you must develop abilities and then develop excellence in the use of these abilities."

—*Rhoda Lachar*

"The life that is unexamined is not worth living."

—*Plato*

TRUE STORY

Laura Kaufmann was an attractive and ambitious young woman who seemed to have everything going for her. What most people didn't know, however, was that she was scared to death to speak in front of people. She feared speaking in meetings and workshops; she even feared speaking to strangers on a one-to-one basis.

Finally, following the advice of her supervisor, Laura decided to overcome her problem. With the help of a communication consultant, she became actively involved in overcoming her anxieties and improving her communication skills.

Today Laura is a senior sales executive and a speaker at numerous conferences. And today, you have begun started working on the plan that changed Laura's life.

---

difficult customer, then you must be competent in other areas too. Effective speaking in front of your boss, colleagues, or customers will lead these individuals to believe that you are a capable and important employee. Giving a speech, explaining instructions to a customer, or discussing your ideas with your supervisor will give you an opportunity to demonstrate your proficiency.

Effective communication is also an ego booster. The more comfortable you feel speaking in front of others, the better you feel about yourself. And an increase in self-esteem is directly related to feeling content with your life and achieving your career goals.

Now that you're convinced of the importance of speaking effectively, it's time to become actively involved in improving your communication abilities. You can begin your path to success by spending a minimum of 20 minutes each day reading this book and working on the quizzes and exercises. The good news is that anyone can improve his or her ability to speak effectively by participating in this 20-step program.

There is one catch, however, and that is that you must *want* to improve your speaking abilities. Successful speaking is guaranteed if you become actively involved in each of the 20 chapters of our process. You can and will learn how to communicate with energy and confidence, bringing you one step closer to achieving your important goals. You'll be more comfortable in all of your relationships and your job, finding that you can make a difference in the workplace.

Now that you have completed the information in this chapter and have made the commitment to participate in our 20-step program, let's begin with a short quiz consisting of two parts. Answer the questions in Part I as honestly as you can. If you need to refer back to the information in this chapter for Part II, please do so. Good luck!

QUIZ

Part I

Respond to each of the following statements with *agree* or *disagree*.

_D_   Statement number 1: I need to eliminate my fear of public speaking.

_A_   Statement number 2: I would like the organization of my thoughts to be clearer.

_A_   Statement number 3: I need to improve my listening skills.

_A_   Statement number 4: My confidence needs improvement.

_A_   Statement number 5: It is important that I make myself more marketable for a job.

_A_   Statement number 6: Communicating at meetings usually makes me feel uncomfortable.

_A_   Statement number 7: I would like to be more comfortable during an important meeting with my boss.

_A_   Statement number 8: I need to be more knowledgeable about body language and verbal delivery.

_A_   Statement number 9: Knowing how to use visual aids would help my speeches.

_D_   Statement number 10: I shy away from conflict situations.

_D_   Statement number 11: I need to learn to give criticism in a constructive manner.

_A_   Statement number 12: People often misinterpret what I've said.

_D_   Statement number 13: I need to learn how to deal with people of cultures different than mine.

_A_   Statement number 14: I would like to increase my vocabulary.

_D_   Statement number 15: I'm afraid to speak up in conversations.

_D_   Statement number 16: I have trouble looking at someone when I talk to them.

_A_   Statement number 17: I usually let others do most of the talking.

_A_   Statement number 18: I have opinions but I don't know how to defend them.

_D_   Statement number 19: When I speak I never use gestures.

_D_   Statement number 20: My boss has suggested that I improve my presentation skills.

Part II

1. Why is effective speaking important in the workplace? _Makes me relay what needs a company has._

2. How will being a more effective communicator affect you? _Makes me think before I speak_

Answer Key

Part I

If you answered *agree* to six or more of the statements, then this book is the perfect tool for you. After completing our 20-step program, you will be able to overcome your anxieties about communicating. You will also learn the basics for organizing and delivering your business presentations with style. In addition, you'll master the art of effective communication on the telephone; at meetings and workshops; and with people of all ethnic backgrounds.

Part II

1. Because you'll spend at least 50% of your time communicating with others in business, your speaking skills must be effective. Your business depends on you to communicate with customers in a clear and coherent manner. You also need to use effective speaking when you relate to your coworkers. Miscommunication in the workplace results in millions of dollars of business losses each year.

2. Effective speaking will help you to perform better in your job and will boost your credibility and your confidence.

NEXT STEP

You've completed Chapter 1—congratulations for making the decision to improve your communication abilities! Move on to Chapter 2, *Creating a Great Impression*, and keep up the good work!

CREATING A GREAT IMPRESSION

Have you ever walked into an unfamiliar post office, department store, library, or dental office and, in a matter of just a few minutes, had a favorable or unfavorable feeling about being there? Did you seem to know almost instinctively that this was or wasn't a place you wanted to visit again? Or have you ever met a stranger and you knew, after only a few minutes, that this was someone you'd like to get to know?

If you answered yes to these questions, then you're like most people. You have experienced a powerful, immediate response to a place or person. Because of this instant feeling that most people have when facing a strange business or person, you must be actively aware of the image that you and your business present.

ONE CANNOT *NOT* COMMUNICATE

In *Contact: The First Four Minutes*, authors Leonard Zunin and Natalie Zunin emphasize the importance of creating a positive first impression.

They say that within the first four minutes of meeting a stranger, you evaluate the person and decide to continue the interaction or to part. First impressions are formed very quickly and stay with us for a long time, acting as filters through which we see everything else we learn about a person or place. You must be aware of the image you and your business are projecting.

In the study of human behavior, there is an adage: "One cannot *not* communicate." Whether you yell or roll your eyeballs, dress in a flamboyant or conventional style, or say nothing at all, you are communicating something to someone. It doesn't matter whether you intend to communicate or not. The way you dress, walk, talk, and in general, present yourself, relays a message to others.

A crucial aspect to the adage, "One cannot *not* communicate," is that the meaning is in the mind of the receiver. If a customer enters a store and an employee stays on the telephone instead of offering assistance, it is the customer who interprets the employee's act as rude. Perhaps the employee is on the phone because of an emergency at home and has no intention of being impolite. The meaning of the act is still interpreted by the customer as unprofessional.

The significance of knowing that you're always sending some kind of message to someone is twofold. First, it means in business that we must be particularly aware of how we relate to people. Second, it means that we must be *receiver conscious*, aware at all times of how our customers will be interpreting our behaviors and practices.

When you give presentations to one person or to a large crowd, you must put yourself in the shoes of your customers, colleagues, supervisors, or any other audience to which you speak. By being conscious of others' perceptions, you will improve the effectiveness of any type of presentation you deliver.

Based on current research on the formation of first impressions, the next section will provide information that can help you put your best foot forward when addressing people for the first time.

POSITIVE FIRST IMPRESSIONS

First and foremost, your clothing does make a difference in how you're perceived. In one recent study, people were asked to rate pictures of business personnel according to their credibility. Inevitably, the people who were dressed in a more professional manner were given the highest ratings, indicating that your clothing does affect your credibility.

REMINDERS FOR A GOOD FIRST IMPRESSION

1. Wear clean, neat clothing and jewelry that are appropriate for your work-place.
2. Be conscious of what you say and do.
3. Exhibit confidence.
4. Address individuals' needs.
5. Think of other people as mirrors for your behavior.
6. Don't state the most important information at the very beginning of your speech.

The most important clothing rule is to wear clean, neat clothes and jewelry that are appropriate for your work environment. Long earrings and a pair of faded jeans may work in an art gallery in Taos, New Mexico, but not at Chase Manhattan Bank in New York. Follow the explicit and implicit clothing codes wherever you work and dress appropriately.

Second, be aware and prepared whenever you present material to one or 100 people. The most common presentation problems include nervousness, failure to relate well to an audience, inadequate preparation, and lack of confident delivery. By being conscious of how you appear to others, you are taking a positive step in eliminating any problems. In the remaining chapters we will discuss techniques for eradicating common presentation problems. For now, however, gaining an awareness of how you present yourself is a step in the right direction.

Third, you should exhibit confidence. People want to work with those in business who believe in their product or service, as well as themselves. One way to boost your confidence is by acting self-assured. This process becomes cyclical as your behavior will have a positive effect on the way you feel and vice versa. The bottom line is that you'll build trust and rapport by acting in a confident manner.

Fourth, make each individual in your audience feel as if you're talking to that person and that person alone. Whether you're a participant in a small meeting or a presenter to a large group, do your very best to make each person feel as if you're relating to that person. By being aware of the benefits of your presentation to your audience, you can customize your examples, language, and content to suit their needs.

TRUE STORY

One place where the power of the first impression is most evident is in the courtroom. Most attorneys will advise their clients on the appropriate clothing, jewelry, and overall demeanor in order to create a positive first impression on the jury.

Some attorneys, in fact, have clothing that clients may borrow to wear in the courtroom. The rationale is that not only are first impressions formed quickly, but they are also difficult to change even when contradictory evidence is presented.

Fifth, if you go into every situation with a positive attitude and an enthusiastic demeanor, you'll be pleased with the type of responses you get from other people. When addressing an audience for the first time, think of their behavior as a mirror of your own. Notice how when you are projecting negativity, the people around you seem to exhibit pessimism.

Finally, wait a few minutes after beginning your presentation to state your most valuable information. People spend the first two minutes interpreting the visual data they receive, so there's the chance that anything heard early in the talk could be forgotten.

RELATING TO YOUR CUSTOMERS

In many situations you will be the only contact a customer has with your business. Studies indicate that customers expect more from a business than just the completion of a transaction. In addition, dissatisfied customers will tell approximately seven other people about their negative experience, and those people will tell others, so it is imperative that each interaction you have be positive.

Customers want to be understood and have their business valued. Fortunately, there are some basic guidelines that will help you to keep your customers satisfied. In addition to being competent and efficient, you need to follow the seven guidelines on the next page for customer satisfaction.

Customer Satisfaction

One of the first things that customers note about effective employees is that they smile and are friendly. In addition to making other people feel good, you will also

REMINDERS FOR KEEPING CUSTOMERS SATISFIED

1. Smile and be friendly.
2. If you can't be friendly, remain neutral.
3. Refer to customers by name.
4. If you don't understand a request, ask questions or paraphrase.
5. Concentrate on what you can do.
6. Focus your attention on your customer.
7. Make sure that your verbal and nonverbal delivery match.

benefit from smiling. Research indicates that just the act of smiling can positively affect both your mood and your behavior. So, get in the habit of looking people in the eyes and smiling.

Second, if you absolutely cannot be friendly, then remain neutral. You should never express anger toward a customer or another employee. The best policy for reacting to an extremely negative situation is to remain calm and silent until you can act in a rational manner. Remarks like, "I understand" and "I would feel the same way" are effective in calming down an irate customer.

Third, refer to your customer by name. People feel complimented when they know that someone knows who they are. Using a customer's full name is a way to convey a personal touch. Only use a customer's first name when the person requests that you do so.

Fourth, ask questions or paraphrase your customer's request if you're not sure what the customer wants. If you have any doubts about a customer's needs, ask for clarification immediately. It's far better to be safe than sorry.

Fifth, focus your end of the conversation on what you can do—not what you can't do. For example, if your store does not carry a particular brand of clothing, you might suggest a similar brand that you do carry. Or if your carpet cleaning business does not use water to clean rugs, you could focus on the advantages of a dry chemical formula.

Sixth, maintain eye contact with your customers and give them your undivided attention. A common complaint that customers make is that employees just don't listen to them. Concentrate on listening to what they want. Focusing on your customers will make a major difference in terms of how they feel they're being treated.

Finally, you must make sure that your nonverbal delivery matches your verbal delivery. If your arms are crossed, you're frowning, and you are saying how glad

WORDS FROM THE WISE

"Satisfied customers almost invariably become active agents for the advancement of the company's business."

—American adage

"A customer doesn't need us, we need him. A customer is not an interruption of our work; he is the purpose of it. A customer is a person who brings us his wants. It is our job to handle them profitably for him and ourselves. A customer is not an outsider to our business; he is a vital part of it."

—C. F. Norton

you are to do business with someone, the message will probably be that you do not value that particular customer.

By incorporating these simple reminders into your behavior, you'll strengthen the bond between you and your customers. And, as you've heard before, this positive relationship can only promote the business you represent.

Well you've done it again! You've finished another chapter and are ready to complete the following exercises and questions. Good luck!

EXERCISES

A. The next time that you complete a transaction at a business, analyze what happened during your interaction with the company's representative. Reflect on what was said or done that was both effective and ineffective. If there was a problem, how did that person handle the situation? Then incorporate the positive aspects of this transaction into the way you deal with customers.

B. The next time you meet a stranger, think critically about the labels you place on that person. Then, if it's possible, initiate a conversation with the stranger and see if your observations remain the same. How long did it take for you to size up this stranger?

Questions

1. What is meant by the adage, "One cannot *not* communicate?"
2. How can you create a positive first impression?
3. What are some important guidelines for keeping your customers satisfied?

Answer Key

1. "One cannot *not* communicate" means that you are always communicating something in the presence of others. If you are standing quietly in an elevator, staring at the numbers, you are communicating that you do not want to be bothered by others. If you are continually rubbing your eyes during an important business meeting, you are communicating that you are tired, or worse, bored. You can communicate something even if you have no intention to do so. Because the meaning of a message is in the mind of the receiver, you are always communicating something, therefore, "one cannot *not* communicate."

2. You can create a positive impression by following these guidelines:
   a. Wear appropriate clothing.
   b. Be conscious of what you say and do.
   c. Be genuinely interested in other people.
   d. Exhibit confidence.
   e. Recognize that other people are mirrors of your behavior.

3. Guarantee effective customer relations by following these guidelines:
   a. Smile and be friendly.
   b. If you can't be nice, be neutral.
   c. Call people by their names.
   d. Make sure you understand their requests.
   e. Concentrate on what your business can do, not on what it can't do.
   f. Match your verbal and nonverbal delivery.

NEXT STEP

You should be proud for finishing this chapter and accomplishing all that you have so far. Continue your commitment and hard work to improve your presentation skills. Move on to Chapter 3, *Overcoming Your Nervousness*. Remember that practice makes perfect and you're on the road to success!

CHAPTER | 3

OVERCOMING YOUR NERVOUSNESS

Few people can speak before an audience without feeling some discomfort. Most people experience stage fright, or what is also called speech anxiety, with symptoms of sweaty palms, trembling hands, a dry mouth, or the old standby, butterflies in the stomach. Some people will not speak in small groups, shy away from interacting with strangers, and go to a great deal of trouble to avoid any physical position where they may be in the direct view of others.

Even celebrities—talk show hosts, singers, politicians—routinely state in interviews that they have had to overcome nervousness. In the *Wall Street Journal* not long ago, a former board chairman of a Forbes 500 company said that what he dreaded most about his job was giving a speech. He also added, however, that if he had never given a speech, he probably would not be where he is today. *Business Communication* published the results of a survey indicating that public speaking was Americans' number one fear. And according to a psychiatry journal, approximately one-third of all people suffer extreme anxiety when asked to address an audience. The bottom line is that everyone is touched to some degree by stage fright, and most people who are successful have learned to channel their fear into enthusiasm for speaking.

There is a simple explanation for communication anxiety. When you are faced with a situation where you're the center of attention and everyone is watching you, your body sends you messages of fright or flight. Shortness of breath is caused by increased heartbeat, clammy hands are a result of lack of circulation, and dryness in your mouth is due to an increased release of sugar. The positive aspect is that we can also explain how to eliminate communication nervousness. By incorporating the following seven steps into your life, you can turn a negative emotional response into a positive experience. So read the following information carefully and know that you're on the path to communicating more effectively.

SEVEN STEPS TO GET RID OF NERVOUSNESS

Step One

The most important thing to do to alleviate nervousness is to use positive thinking and focus on success. All of us communicate to ourselves. We are constantly conducting intrapersonal communication, or *self-talk*, in our heads. We give ourselves information about someone or something, we judge our friends and relatives, we record reminders to ourselves, and we constantly evaluate ourselves and our abilities.

The best way to become comfortable speaking to others is to become aware of what you say to ourselves, replacing any negative thoughts with positive self-talk. Remind yourself of the positive results you will achieve when you accomplish a speaking task. Tell yourself that you can do almost anything you set your mind to do. When you make any attempt at improving your speaking abilities, pat yourself on the back and reinforce yourself with more positive self-talk.

Positive reinforcement will do a great deal to improve your self-confidence. A former chairperson of a large corporation once said that "believing you can get self-esteem from someone else is a trap. There are no external solutions to internal problems." Or as Eleanor Roosevelt once said, "No one can make you feel inferior without your consent."

Any time you are thinking something negative about yourself or your speaking abilities, change that thought to a positive one and know that you are taking action. Stop putting yourself down out loud or inside your head. Replace *can't* with *can* and *won't* with *will*.

You won't acquire total self-confidence overnight, but it will happen. One single act of confidence breeds a feeling of self-assurance that in turn breeds more and more acts of confidence. Try positive thinking and watch your self-confidence increase, your nervousness diminish, and your speaking skills blossom.

Step Two

Second, it's important to achieve a relaxed state through breathing exercises. Breathing is important to health and healing because how we breathe affects our nervous systems. You can alter your heart rate, circulation, and other bodily functions by changing the beat and deepness of your breath. Andrew Weil, M.D., the best-selling author of *Spontaneous Healing*, recommends taking relaxing breaths every morning and evening and in stressful situations (such as at public presentations).

A *relaxing breath* begins with the tip of your tongue placed against the soft tissue between the teeth and the roof of your mouth. Exhale completely through your mouth, while you make an audible sound. Next, close your mouth and inhale quietly through the nose to a silent count of four. Hold the breath for a count of seven. Then exhale audibly through the mouth to a count of eight. Repeat for a total of four cyles, then breathe normally.

This exercise can be altered a bit by changing your location; sitting with your back straight, standing, or walking. A relaxing breath can become part of your daily ritual, assisting you to become more centered and less anxious about communicating.

Step Three

Third, you must realize that your audience will be much kinder and gentler than you anticipate. People want you to succeed. They want to learn something, be touched, or be motivated by your talk. As a result, audiences are not going to be as critical of you as you are of yourself.

In most speaking situations, people do not even know that a speaker is nervous. Unless you pass out or continually say, "I'm sooooo nervous," your audience will probably never notice your feelings of anxiety. It's amazing how many seemingly calm television talk show hosts are actually quite anxious before talking to millions of people on air. The key is that they have learned to channel their nervousness into enthusiasm and energy; so can you.

Step Four

Fourth, you need to realize that the best speakers are not acting, but rather being themselves and being human. You will not be effective if you try to put on airs or pretend to be someone you are not. Maximize your own personal style by relating to others in a down-to-earth, heartfelt style.

A significant aspect of relating to your audience is to forget about yourself. Focus on your subject matter and your audience. Instead of spending your time wondering how you're coming across, concentrate on whether your listeners are understanding your message. As a public speaker, you need to be most concerned about your audience and the message they're receiving.

Step Five

Fifth, take charge of your speaking situation. Audiences want to listen to someone who is in control, so incorporate a confident demeanor into your delivery. Pause before you begin your speech, and then use short sentences in your introduction.

Go slowly in order to get your bearings and never include statements such as, "I really wish I wasn't giving this speech," or "I hate being in front of you today." Recognize your responsibility of speaking in front of a group, relish the opportunity to improve and increase your self-confidence, and assist your audience in understanding your information.

Step Six

Sixth, use an outline of the main points of your speech. Never write out your speech word-for-word because it would tempt you to spend all of your time looking at your written text instead of looking at your audience. Write short sentences or phrases of the most important items in your talk. It will help to number each point with a roman numeral (I, II, III, etc.). Then, when you are speaking, you can briefly glance down at your main points and still concentrate on relating to your audience.

Step Seven

The final point is crucial: Spend time on the preparation and rehearsal of your talk. It's been estimated that a speaker should spend about 60% of his or her total invested time on the preparation and rehearsal of a speech. Practice delivering

REMINDERS FOR ELIMINATING NERVOUSNESS

1. Replace any negative self-talk with positive reinforcement. Tell yourself you can and will succeed. Confidence is a strong motivator.
2. Practice breathing techniques to increase your relaxation.
3. Remember that your audience is not there to criticize and condemn, but to learn and appreciate.
4. Relate to your audience in a down-to-earth manner. Save your acting skills for plays.
5. Begin your speech slowly with short sentences. Avoid negative comments such as, "I don't know anything about this," or "I wish I wasn't speaking today."
6. Use a brief outline with your major points written as sentences or phrases.
7. Implement the three P's-practice, practice, and more practice.

your outlined speech in front of a mirror or to a friend or relative. You can self-evaluate your own speech by videotaping or audiotaping your presentation. Because people generally are their own worst critics, lighten up and you'll probably be delighted to see and hear that you're a much better speaker than you thought you would be.

Recognize the importance of the three P's: practice, practice, and more practice. Just as you move your muscles to increase your strength, so must you take every opportunity to speak in front of others to improve your speaking abilities. You learned to walk by walking, to read by reading, to drive by driving, and you'll improve your public speaking by speaking. Great speakers are not born, but rather trained through practice.

Great work so far! Now, apply the information in this chapter by completing the following exercises and questions. And of course, integrate this material into your professional life.

EXERCISES

A. Record your negative self-talk over a period of a week. Every time you catch yourself being too self-critical or negative, stop, write down the comment, and then record and think of a positive comment about you. For instance, if you realize that you're thinking that you can't possibly go in and talk to

WORDS FROM THE WISE

"When speaking, concentrate on the subject of the talk. Forget all about yourself, like a soldier going over the top."

—*Manly Hall*

"If you think you can, you can. If you think you can't, you're probably right."

—*Mary Kay, Mary Kay Cosmetics*

your boss, stop and write that thought down. Then record and remind yourself that you most certainly can speak to your boss! If you find that you are thinking that you did a terrible job speaking at a conference, your notebook would have an entry like the following. After a period of one week, you should see an improvement in the way you think about yourself and in your confidence level. After a week of recording your self-talk, continue this exercise informally and note how positive self-talk is directly associated with a positive self-concept.

DATE	REPLACE NEGATIVE	WITH POSITIVE
May 1	I did a terrible job speaking.	I did my best, and everyone clapped.

B. Practice the relaxing breath (page 17 of this chapter) every night for a week and before any stressful communication. Your objective in doing this exercise is to become calmer and thus more capable of accomplishing any challenge. After one week, continue the exercise when you're faced with a difficult speaking situation or any other problem.

C. The next time you are in a meeting, listening to a speech, or attending a seminar or conference, note your attitude toward the speaker. More than likely your disposition will be positive and you'll want the speaker to succeed. Like most audience members, you'll want to learn something and benefit from listening. After you have completed this exercise and the next time you give a speech, remember your attitude toward the speaker in this exercise and recognize that your audience will, more than likely, be supportive of *you.*

D. The next time you watch the news on television, listen very carefully and record the main points of each segment. Use roman numerals; write down only the major points, not every word. This exercise will give you practice in both outlining and listening. With this practice, writing outlines should become much easier.

QUIZ

1. Discuss five ways to overcome speech anxiety.
2. Use roman numerals in an outline format to identify the three main points in the following paragraph.

When I was little, I loved to sell lemonade at a stand. I spent almost every summer day at the lemonade stand, making and selling more than 30 glasses each day. In my teens, I traveled door to door, selling magazines. By the end of 11th grade, I had made more than $10,000, met hundreds of new people, and decided what I would do with my life. Now that I'm in my late 20s, I am still selling. I am the senior executive sales accountant for a computer company. I love what I do, and I still look back on my lemonade stand with the fondest of memories.

3. What is negative self-talk and why is it important to replace it with positive thoughts?

Answer Key

1. Some of the most effective ways to eliminate speech anxiety are the following:
   a. Use only positive self-talk.
   b. Practice calm breathing.
   c. Recognize that audiences are generally supportive.
   d. Concentrate on a personal delivery.
   e. Begin slowly and use short, simple sentences.
   f. Use an outline.
   g. Always prepare and practice, practice, practice.
2. Your outline would look something like this:
   I.   As a child, I loved spending my summers working in a lemonade stand.
   II. When I was an adolescent, I was very successful selling magazines.
   III. Now that I'm in my 20s, I am a senior sales executive.

3. Negative self-talk is the nonproductive thinking we do that can limit our growth and self-confidence. It is full of negative criticism of ourselves and what we can accomplish. Negative self-talk makes us think that we can't accomplish something or that we can never get over our anxieties. By replacing negative self-talk with positive affirmations, we can accomplish almost anything we set our minds to, thereby improving our self-confidence and becoming more successful. It's important to replace thoughts like, "I'll never be able to speak in front of a group" with positive thoughts such as, "I know I can accomplish speaking to an audience."

NEXT STEP

Now that you've completed Chapter 3, pat yourself on the back, continue your positive self-talk, and move on to Chapter 4, *Considering Your Audience.*

CHAPTER | 4

CONSIDERING YOUR AUDIENCE

Most inexperienced speechmakers are quite surprised to find that different audiences react differently to the same information. First-year managers or customer service representatives commonly remark that the same presentation was a hit with one group of people and a bomb with another. After gaining some experience, these speakers recognize audience characteristics and learn to incorporate the art of audience analysis into the creation of an effective speech for every audience.

Audience analysis is defining who your listeners are and what perceptions they may have about your subject. Audience analysis also involves examining the environment in which your speech will be given. Using audience analysis techniques, you can tailor your presentation specifically for the most important audience—the one you are facing next.

WHO IS YOUR AUDIENCE?

Who are the people who will be listening to you talk? Do you work with them? Are they potential or current customers? Are they supervisors, or are they the owners of your business? The more clear and specific you can be about who these listeners are, the easier it will be to design a message suited for their needs. Ultimately, you want your audience to understand and accept what you have to say; therefore, the more you can adapt your speech to fit their needs, the better your chances are for success.

Theodore Sorensen, speechwriter for President Kennedy, stated in his book *Kennedy* that the most important aspects of speechwriting were the audience's comprehension and comfort. Follow the lead of famous and successful speech-writers and design your presentation to suit your audience. Make your ideas easy to understand, and keep your listeners comfortable as they assess what you have to say.

Once you define your audience, you'll be able to use examples, language, and concepts that can best reach them. Eventually, you will get to the point where defining your audience will become second nature, but for now, use the following list of questions to assist you in determining whom you'll be reaching.

QUESTIONS ABOUT YOUR AUDIENCE

How many people will there be—10, 20, or 100? The number will determine how loud you need to talk, what kind of special arrangements need to be made for seating and sound, and the type of audiovisual aids you will use.

Are they men, women, or a mixture of both? The gender of your audience can influence what kind of examples you use. Although you want to be careful about generalizing, some examples may elicit stronger reactions in certain audiences. For example, stories about single parenting or sexual harassment would be pertinent to both genders, whereas a story about insurance coverage for postpartum hospital stays would appeal to a female audience.

What does your audience know about your subject? You don't want to bore them by telling them what they already know, but at the same time, you must never confuse them by assuming that their knowledge is greater than it actually is.

Do they speak a particular jargon or do they know complex technical information? You may need to create a handout or other audiovisual aid explaining technical facts or information that is only used by your business.

How long will you be speaking to the group? The difference between preparing for a five-minute speech and a thirty-minute talk would be about 3,000 words.

What does the audience expect from you? At the end of your talk, are they supposed to be informed about or be proficient in creating a profit-and-loss sheet? Knowing what your audience expects will enable you to incorporate valuable information into your talk.

What do they have that you want? Be clear about what you want to achieve as a result of your talk. Do you want a job? Do you want money for a product? Or is having a satisfied customer reward enough for your talk?

Knowing the answers to these questions can make a major difference in creating a message that is both beneficial and interesting for your audience.

Define Your Audience

1. How many people will be in your audience?
2. Are they male, female, or a mixture of both?
3 What do they know about your subject?
4. Do they use a particular jargon?
5. How long will you be speaking?
6. What do they expect or want from you?
7. What do you want from your audience?

PERCEPTION

As you do more and more public speaking, you'll learn that one person's interpretation of a speech may be entirely different from another's. Researchers say this is because of differences in perception. *Perception* is how we view the world, both what we see and how we interpret what we see. Our perceptions are based on where and how we were brought up, and what we learned from our guardians, friends, and educational experiences.

The perceptions you have are reflected in your behavior. If you think that everyone is out to get you, then you may act in a defensive manner that will probably alienate people. As speakers, we must be open and positive, realizing that not everyone views the world as we do. It is important to try to understand where members of your audience are coming from; that is, to put yourself in their shoes. A good speaker will treat an audience with respect, even if the views of the individuals in the audience do not match the speaker's own beliefs.

Here is an extremely valuable idea to remember: How your audience *perceives* your message is the key to any presentation. Ultimately, it doesn't matter what your intentions are—your audience's perception will determine whether you are successful. Therefore, being conscious of the perceptions of your audience will assist you in creating a speech that will affect them in the way you want.

SHORT TALKS AND FORMAL PRESENTATIONS

Most people in the workplace are responsible for giving thousands of short, impromptu presentations to customers and colleagues each year. These presentations range from a brief conversation about a bill to a five-minute tutorial on the use of a computer.

It has been estimated that each year the average worker in America gives approximately fifteen formal presentations to colleagues, customers, and supervisors. These talks may last from five minutes to one hour and involve more extensive preparation.

Whether you are required to give one or 100 informal or formal presentations each year, you'll need to master the art of speaking effectively. If oral communication is an important aspect of your position, find out what type of presentations you are required to give. In addition to considering your audience, define the length and type of the presentation itself. The following information will help you to categorize the types of business presentations you may be expected to deliver.

You'll need to know whether you are to deliver a short or long speech. Short talks range from one to about 10 minutes in length. These are generally periodic, brief reports, condensed programs, or committee updates that must be organized, succinct, and clear. Short talks may run the gamut from an introduction of new employees at a team meeting to a short speech of explanation about how a new fax machine works.

Long or formal presentations may vary from 10 minutes to one hour. Many conferences, businesses, and organizations have a time limit of approximately 30

WORDS FROM THE WISE

"You need to research your audience first and then organize your speech in terms your audience can understand and relate to."

—*Betty Heitman, former co-chair of the Republican National Committee*

minutes for speeches. Long oral reports or proposals that summarize written materials are commonly presented within many organizations. These formal presentations restate the significant points that are detailed in an end-of-the-year report, marketing plan, or sales projection proposal. Long talks are also frequently scheduled at regional, national, or international conferences of businesses, and professional, or political organizations. These presentations range from research to controversial issues.

KINDS OF BUSINESS PRESENTATIONS

Both short and long talks are generally broken into the following five categories: public relations, instruction, briefings, reports, and persuasive communication. We'll provide an overview of each type of presentation.

- **Public relations speeches** promote good will and positive feelings about a business. Most large companies understand the value of maintaining positive relationships with stockholders, customers, politicians, and the public at large. Many companies provide speakers' bureaus where employees are available to speak to the public. Coors Brewing Company in Golden, Colorado, maintains a speakers' bureau of employees who address many issues such as drinking and driving; succeeding in the corporate environment; and overcoming major obstacles in one's life. Coors sponsors these speakers at no cost in order to foster positive relations with the community. Other public relations speeches include introductions, bestowing awards, and welcome and farewell talks. The mood of public relations talks is generally upbeat and positive.
- The **instructional speech** can be either formal or informal. Your goal in this type of talk is for your audience to understand the material you are covering and to apply your explanation to their work. For example, you could explain how an indexing system works, the correct procedure for filing a complaint, or the most effective way to handle customers. The important part of this kind of speech is to make sure that your audience can adequately apply what you've told them.
- A **briefing** is a session where information is provided to a decision maker so that eventually a problem may be solved or a decision will be made. Generally a briefing will consist of background material, the options available, the pros and cons of the options, and any other information that will assist a

leader in solving a problem. Here is an illustration: Before making a public statement about a city ruling on her billboard company, the CEO of the business called a staff briefing. The CEO's employees informed her about the background and consequences of the new city ruling that limited the number of billboards; the positive and negative consequences of making certain statements about the ruling; and how council members and the community felt about the limitations. The briefing assisted the CEO in making a public statement that would indicate the company's position without alienating the community.

- **Reports** are an extremely common type of speech in most businesses. Some employees are responsible for weekly or monthly updates on the progress of their projects at staff meetings. Reports give everyone in a department or staff an opportunity to find out what's happening in all areas of their division or company. Reports can cover topics that run the gamut from the progress in gaining prospective clients to the problems with integrating a new computer system.

- The **persuasive speech** has the purpose of getting others to accept your opinion or idea and generally involves others changing their view of something. Let's say that you have developed a great marketing idea and you know that your plan could increase sales of your business's products. It's up to you to create a persuasive speech, explaining your plan and providing evidence that will support your belief that the business will profit. Or perhaps you are convinced that your business can save hours each week by making two changes in your bookkeeping system. Your task in a persuasive speech is to present what you want to change and to support your argument with substantiated evidence.

THE SALES SPEECH

A unique and highly valued kind of persuasive talk is the sales speech. People who master sales can be some of the best-paid individuals in business. Because the important characteristics of a sales speech remain the same no matter what you are selling, salespeople are able to transfer their skills from business to business. Thus, there is a lot of freedom that comes from mastering the sales speech.

Research indicates that there are four components fundamental to the sales speech. These areas include sincerity, empathy, knowledge, and enthusiasm. **Sincerity** involves a belief in both what you're selling and the benefits of that product

REMINDERS FOR AN EFFECTIVE SALES SPEECH

1. Be sincere.
2. Express empathy.
3. Be knowledgeable.
4. Show enthusiasm.

or service for the buyer. If you're not honest, it's difficult to look someone in the eye and list the reasons why someone needs what you offer.

Empathy is another important aspect of the sales speech. Empathy is an emotional response that you can feel with another person. When you can truly understand the perceptions of another person, then you can empathize with him or her. Empathy enables you to comprehend why a particular product or service is important to someone. This understanding provides the basis for establishing the benefits of your product or service.

Knowledge is key in any sales speech. For most buyers, knowledge is equated with credibility, and credibility is related to confidence in a business's product or service. The more you know about your company, the product or service, and the competition, the more convincing you will be.

The fourth characteristic of an effective sales speech is **enthusiasm.** When salespeople exhibit a zest for life and their product or service, buyers become excited about the benefits they may receive. Almost everyone likes to shake up their daily routine, and a sales speech that provides a bit of excitement helps a potential buyer to experience something different.

Persuasive talks, and particularly sales speeches, are considered a bit more difficult than the other kinds of speeches because your objective is not only to inform your audience about a subject, but more importantly, to convince people to accept your point of view. The rewards, however, can be extremely beneficial if you get that raise you're requesting or you succeed in getting a new account.

Whenever you are requested to give a talk, make sure that you analyze your audience and are aware of the type of presentation you are to give. Being prepared for differences in audiences and business presentations will help you to be specific in preparing your talk.

The following exercises will aid you in incorporating the information from this chapter into your life.

WORDS FROM THE WISE

"Confidence and enthusiasm are the great sales producers."

—*Alfred Armand Montapert*

"A man can succeed at almost anything for which he has unlimited enthusiasm."

—*Charles Schwab*

EXERCISES

A. At the next few speeches you attend, define the audience and the kind of talk that is given. This exercise will help you when it is time to analyze your own audience.

B. Think of someone you know who seems quite different than you. Record what you think contributed to the differences in the way you two view the world. Next, write down some things you want in life and some items the other person wants. Examine your lists and think about the way our perceptions are formed and the impact such perceptions have on our lives. The next time you give a speech, reflect on how individuals in the audience may view your subject matter, depending on their individual goals and perceptions.

C. When you interact with salespeople, analyze them according to their knowledge, sincerity, empathy, and enthusiasm. Did they persuade you to purchase a product or service? What was effective and ineffective in their sales speech? How could you have improved what they said or did?

QUIZ

1. What are five questions that will help you define your audience?
2. What is perception? Why is perception so important when you are giving a speech?
3. Explain five kinds of business speeches.
4. What are four essentials of a sales speech?

Answer Key

1. Ask the following questions about your audience:

   a. Are they males, females, or a mixture of both?

   b. Should you use jargon or other technical language?

   c. What will be the length of your speech?

   d. What does the audience expect from you?

   e. What do you expect to get from the audience?

2. Perception is how an individual views the world. Our perception of a speech may vary, dependent on our education and socialization. Perception is important in speechmaking because the true test of a speech is not what the speaker intends, but what the audience perceives.

3. Business speeches can be categorized as follows:

   a. Public relations

   b. Instruction

   c. Briefings

   d. Reports

   e. Persuasive communication

4. An effective sales speech entails sincerity, empathy, knowledge, and enthusiasm.

NEXT STEP

Congratulations on completing Chapter 4! Move on to Chapter 5, *Knowing Your Purpose*, and remember that an effective learning experience involves application of knowledge into your life. Keep up the good work!

CHAPTER | 5

KNOWING YOUR PURPOSE

Most of us have sat through long, drawn-out speeches at work. We've listened to reports or briefings and wondered what the point was. As we all know from personal experience, it can be extremely frustrating, not to mention boring, when someone is speaking and you haven't a clue where they're headed. There's no quicker way to lose a customer or alienate a potential buyer than by rambling and not saying anything of use.

As a speaker, one of your most important tasks is to define your purpose for speaking. It is not the responsibility of your audience to sort through your presentation, trying to figure out the objective. It's up to you to clearly define what you're speaking about. When you speak, just as when you write, you must know your purpose. As the old adage goes, "If you don't know where you're headed, you'll probably end up somewhere else." So know where you're going.

GENERAL PURPOSE

Each talk that you give will have a general and a specific purpose. The three general purposes in speechmaking are to inform, to persuade, and to entertain. Let's examine each type.

- An **informative** speech is an instructional and unbiased talk that is designed to increase your audience's knowledge about a particular subject. Your report on last year's refrigerator sales or your introduction of new employees would be examples of informative speeches. In informative speeches you present your material as a teacher does, without bias and with an objective of educating the audience.

- A **persuasive** speech's primary intent is to change the views, opinions, or behaviors of an audience. Persuasive speeches in business are generally designed to get the audience to accept an opinion or buy a product or service. There are many situations in business when you want to motivate your audience with a persuasive speech in hope that, in time, the motivation will be reflected in good will or sales.

  For example, you might give a speech to persuade your audience that your department is the best in the company. Your persuasive speech will motivate the audience to have a positive attitude toward the business which will result in more sales. In persuasive speeches, you could persuade an audience to buy your product or motivate a group of Amway dealers to believe in the effectiveness of the new line of cleaning solvents. The bottom line in a persuasive speech is that, as a result of your talk, you want people to make a change.

- An **entertaining** speech results in enjoyment and lifted spirits. Entertaining speeches are humorous, comprising jokes, illustrations, and stories. Generally, entertaining speeches occur at social events, such as an award gala or a banquet for key sales personnel. Your entertaining speech should keep the audience interested and amused.

While informative, persuasive, and entertaining speeches have three distinct purposes, you may have overlapping objectives in certain speeches. There's certainly nothing wrong with adding some information to your entertaining speech. And more likely than not, you will probably sell more of your product if you include humor in your persuasive speech. Just make sure that if your goal is to persuade, you don't spend all of your time entertaining, at the cost of a sale.

> # THREE GENERAL PURPOSES
>
> 1. Informative
> 2. Persuasive
> 3. Entertaining

SPECIFIC PURPOSE

Once you know the general purpose of your speech, you can combine it with information about your subject in order to create your specific purpose. The specific purpose is not only the central idea and objective of your speech, but also the response you want your audience to have.

Let's say that you have been asked to show three new employees how to use the fax machine. Your specific purpose would be: To inform my audience how to follow five steps in using the fax machine. Note that you will, of course, be giving an informative speech. You have included "my audience" in the specific purpose so that you will carefully consider your audience when preparing your talk. Moreover, you have focused on the topic—five steps in using the fax machine—so that your subject will be clear, easy to follow, and manageable in the time you have been allotted.

Or perhaps you have been assigned to give a speech to prospective customers. Your specific purpose could be: to persuade my audience of the two major benefits of enrolling in our health plan. By establishing your specific purpose, you know: 1) that you are speaking to persuade, 2) that you are aware that your audience is made up of prospective customers, and 3) that you will emphasize the two most important benefits of enrolling. Your specific purpose will help you to be clear about what you're presenting and what you expect the outcome to be.

> # EXAMPLES OF SPECIFIC PURPOSES
>
> *Informative*—To inform my audience about the three bonus benefits of the Sunshine Healthcare package.
>
> *Persuasive*—To persuade my audience to join the Pro Health Club.
>
> *Entertaining*—To entertain my audience with anecdotes about working with Bob.

When you are planning your speeches, you'll also need to consider time. You can cover approximately two points in five minutes. Don't try to cover too much information in a limited amount of time; on the other hand, you shouldn't search for fill-ins to cover for a lack of information.

Before you decide on a speech topic, make sure that 1) you have an adequate amount of information for the subject, and 2) that the subject you're considering fits the requirements of the speaking engagement. There's nothing worse than not having any information on a topic or selecting a topic that your boss doesn't like.

DELIVERY STYLES

Once you have sized up your audience and you know what your specific purpose will be, you'll need to consider the style of delivery for your speech. The four styles of delivery are impromptu, manuscript, memorized, and extemporaneous. Each style has its merits and drawbacks. Let's examine each.

- **Impromptu** speaking is the most spontaneous of the four styles of speech-making. It involves speaking on the spur of the moment without advance preparation. Let's say you're at your departmental meeting and your boss asks you to tell the rest of the group what you've been working on. You have to respond in a spontaneous manner without any notes or preparation. Of course, the more familiar you are with the information, the easier it will be to give an impromptu speech.

  When you're delivering the speech, always concentrate on being organized, coherent, and clear. And remember that, while it may be uncomfortable at first to speak on an impromptu basis, the more practice you have, the better speaker you will become. In fact, it may be to your best advantage to volunteer for impromptu speeches (especially when you are well-versed on the topic). The more practice you have speaking, the better your skills will become, and in turn, the better your job performance will be.

- For many politicians, CEOs, and newscasters the **manuscript** speech is the preferred method of delivery. This is because a manuscript speech is planned and written out word-for-word. Since most politicians, CEOs, and newscasters don't write their own copy, they must depend on a verbatim script. In addition, because of the importance and impact of their speeches, politicians, CEOs, and newscasters must be flawless in their delivery of each foreign name, technical term, or difficult concept.

FOUR DELIVERY STYLES

1. Impromptu
2. Manuscript
3. Memorized
4. Extemporaneous

For most of us, however, the manuscript style gets in the way of our ability to deliver a natural and relaxed speech. There are times during a speech when we may incorporate the manuscript style to relate a complex technical definition or a quotation from the president of our company. But for the most part, the manuscript style of delivery is not encouraged.

- The **memorized** style of delivery is one where you rehearse your speech over and over until it is committed to memory. The major drawback of this style is that if you happen to forget one section of your speech, you may end up ruining your whole message. It may be in your best interest to memorize a few beginning and ending sentences of your speech. That way you can really concentrate on eye contact with your audience at the most crucial times of your speech.

- **Extemporaneous** speaking is the style you will probably become most familiar with. Extemporaneous speaking involves preparation, use of an outline or brief notes during a speech, and a relaxed and comfortable delivery that seems conversational in nature. Extemporaneous speaking is the best style for relating to your audience and giving each audience member the impression that you are talking to them as individuals.

REASON, CREDIBILITY, AND EMOTION

No matter what style of delivery you use, there are three characteristics that every effective speech must have. These are the qualities of reason, credibility, and emotion. Over 2,000 years ago, the noted philosopher Aristotle said that every great speech must use logic to make people think and emotion to make people feel. Aristotle also emphasized that the speaker must possess a credible demeanor in order for the audience to respect and believe what is said. What Aristotle said is as true today as it was 2,000 years ago.

> ### THREE IMPORTANT ASPECTS OF A PRESENTATION
>
> 1. Reason
> 2. Credibility
> 3. Emotion

If you are requested to persuade a group of prospective investors to purchase stock in your company, you'll need to provide concrete reasons, enthusiasm that the stocks will increase in value over time, and a demeanor that you know what you're talking about. Reason, emotion, and credibility have endured as essential characteristics of effective speeches.

THE MAIN POINTS OF YOUR SPEECH

Once you know who your audience is, your specific purpose, the type of presentation, and delivery style for your speech, you can begin to work on the nuts and bolts of your talk. This step involves gathering and then organizing the main points of your speech.

Imagine that your boss has asked you to give a 10-minute speech to introduce Mr. Success, a guest speaker, at your next departmental meeting. By examining his biographical sheet and talking to a few fellow employees, you know that Mr. Success has written three bestselling books on small business ownership, has received more than 50 governmental and private sector awards for his philanthropic contributions, and has turned an initial investment of $5,000 into a million-dollar company in less than 10 years.

In addition, you have gathered additional information for each of these three main points. You know that his first business was a direct-mail company started in the garage of his home. And you've learned the titles of all his books and the types of awards he received. Gathering all of this information will enable you to substantiate the three main points of your speech.

You also recognize that in 10 minutes, you can adequately address the specific purpose: to inform your audience about Mr. Success's three major accomplishments. In consideration of your audience, which is composed of businesspeople, you've decided to arrange the order of main points in order of importance to them.

Therefore, your first main point will be about Mr. Success's million-dollar business. When you create an outline for the main points of your speech, it would look like the following:

Outlining Your Main Points

Mr. Success: A Role Model for Achievement

Specific Purpose: To inform my audience about Mr. Success's three major accomplishments.

I. Mr. Success turned an initial investment of $5,000 into a million-dollar business.
   A. He started his direct-mail business in his garage.
   B. After 10 years and three restructures of the business, the company's net worth is $10 million.
II. Mr. Success is also a bestselling author.
   A. He has written three books, *What It Takes To Be a Millionaire*, *Follow The Rainbow*, and *Start In Your Garage*.
   B. Mr. Success consults with CEOs around the world.
III. Mr. Success has also received numerous governmental and private sector awards for his philanthropic contributions.
   A. He was named The Most Generous Entrepreneur, The Prince of Business Contributors, and The Man Who Cares by various business organizations.
   B. Mr. Success has established a fund for inner-city youth who want to go to college but are unable to afford school.

If your specific purpose is to persuade your audience to use your company's credit card, then you'll need to come up with the main reasons why someone should buy your card instead of another.

Let's say that you have the following four reasons why your card is the one to purchase: 1) There is no interest fee for the first six months, 2) All transfers of other credit card balances are free, 3) You'll receive a free $100 gift certificate to Macy's for joining, and 4) No one (that's right, no one!) is refused a credit card.

As you record the preceding four reasons, you'll also need to write down additional information about each point. For example, you may want to establish that after six months the APR is only 9.9%! And when you discuss free transferability

WORDS FROM THE WISE

Success, remember, is the reward of toil.

—Sophocles

of current accounts, you can make sure to verify that the process can take place over the phone. It's always a good idea to have at least two sentences of support for each of your main points.

When you have your main points written down, then you'll need to arrange them in an order that will be the most persuasive for your audience. If you are trying to persuade a group of college students or first-time credit card users, then you should probably begin your main points with the fact that *No one is refused a credit card.* If you're addressing an audience who "shops around" for credit values, then the best bet is to begin with the main point of *No interest fee for the six months.* You'll need to know your audience so that you can organize your main points in the most effective manner.

The outline of your main points when presented to college students may look like the following:

The Credit Card for You

Specific Purpose: To persuade my audience of the four reasons they should apply for BankTen's Credit Card.

I. Everyone is accepted for a BankTen Credit Card.
   A. The only requirement is that you are 21 years of age.
   B. No matter what your credit history is, you'll receive a BankTen credit card.
II. You'll even receive a $100 gift certificate from Macy's department store.
   A. You can use the money to buy something or pay on your account.
   B. You can spend the certificate within the next two years.
III. There is no interest on your charges for the next six months.
   A. Your balance will only reflect the charges you have made.
   B. After six months your APR will be only 9.9%.
IV. At any time you can transfer other credit card balances at no cost.
   A. You can open other accounts and transfer the balance so that you don't have to pay any interest.

B. The balance transfer offer also applies to department stores and shopping channel charges.

By now you are probably able to see how your main points are the essence of your speech. You'll need to spend some time preparing your major points and the elaboration of these points. Now take some time continue in this chapter with the following exercises and questions.

EXERCISES

A. The next time you attend a speech in person or watch a speech being given on television, analyze the talk according to the following criteria: 1) What was the specific purpose of the speech, 2) What style of delivery was used, 3) What were the main points, and 4) Were reason, credibility, and emotion incorporated into the speech?

B. As you listen to a coworker or friend, mentally make note of their main points. Even in a friendly conversation, people establish major points as they speak. Also listen for further elaboration on these main points. Listening for main points will demonstrate the importance of being clear and coherent for your audience.

Quiz

1. Why is it important to have a specific purpose when you're speaking?
2. Explain the four styles of delivery.
3. Aristotle emphasized three essentials of an effective speech. What are they?

Answer Key

1. A specific purpose will keep you focused on the objective you want to achieve. It will assist you in developing the main points in a speech and prevent you from rambling.
2. The four types of delivery include:
   a. Impromptu
   b. Manuscript
   c. Memorized
   d. Extemporaneous

3. Aristotle's three essentials for a speech include:
    a. Reason
    b. Credibility
    c. Emotion

NEXT STEP

Great work on finishing this chapter! You should be proud of your success so far! Carry on your diligent work with Chapter 6, *Creating a Beginning, Middle, and End.*

CHAPTER | 6

CREATING A BEGINNING, MIDDLE, AND END

A very popular adage recurs in public speaking books and courses: "Telling an audience what you're going to tell them, then tell them what you're telling them, and finally, never forget to tell them what you've already told them." The significance of this saying is that you must be responsible for assuring the audience's comprehension and retention of your message.

Guide your audience in understanding and remembering what you say by organizing your speech into a beginning, middle, and end. Just as you do when you write, you must develop your speech's introduction, body, and conclusion. Studies have shown that organizing your speech into three parts will result in better comprehension for your audience and higher credibility ratings for you as a speaker. Let's examine each of these three parts of a speech, beginning with the introduction.

INTRODUCTION

A lot of research has been conducted in the area of human memory. One recent study indicates that people have a tendency to remember best what they heard first or last in a speech. Consequently, you must create an engaging and instructional introduction and conclusion so that your audience will remember, at the very least, what you said your speech was going to be about and what you said it was about.

When creating an introduction you need to include two elements. First, you must include something that entices and interests your audience to continue listening. Second, you need to embody your specific purpose, telling your audience what the speech is about.

Let's say that you have been asked to speak at the national conference of your administrative assistants' union. Your specific purpose is to inform your audience about the three most innovative and beneficial technologies affecting an office today. Your audience will consist of administrative assistants who, like you, are members of the union. A relatively dry opening for your speech might be something like the following:

> Hello, everyone. Thanks for attending my session on innovative and beneficial technologies. I'll begin by talking about the latest technology that has been incorporated into our offices at IBM.

Perhaps a more effective introduction might be something like this.

> Good morning and welcome. Thanks for giving me the opportunity to address you again. Let me begin my speech today with a thought-provoking statement. Within the next 10 years, office technology will be so advanced that

WORDS FROM THE WISE

"The secret of public speaking: It's easy, all you have to do is think up a good beginning, next, you think up a good closing. Then you keep the two as close together as possible."

—*Grenville Kleiser*

80% of our responsibilities as administrative assistants could be handled by computers! What this means to everyone in this room is that we must be aware of and become competent in using the latest technologies. Because if we don't, our services could become outdated. Today I am here to start you down the path of technological mastery. Over the next 40 minutes I will be explaining the three most current and innovative inventions for the office. Listen carefully and know that the information you receive will help your skills today, as well as save your job tomorrow.

You would probably agree that the second introduction was quite a bit more interesting than the first. At the same time, the second introduction was very specific in stating the purpose of the speech and establishing two strong benefits for listening to the speech.

There are four tried-and-true techniques that speechwriters use again and again to secure the attention of an audience. These methods include using a rhetorical question, statistic, quotation, or story. Let's begin by discussing a rhetorical question.

Rhetorical Question

A rhetorical question is asked to motivate your audience to think about a particular topic. When you begin your speech with "How many people in this room know what they need to be financially prepared for retirement?" you don't want everyone to yell out their answer or for someone to take a quick personal survey of audience members. You just want your audience to begin thinking about and become interested in the topic. Then you can proceed with your speech about becoming financially independent by retirement.

Imagine that you were assigned to give a talk on the financial benefits of owning a home. Your introduction might be something like this:

Do you realize that every year you could be throwing away more than $1,000 in tax benefits? If you're renting your primary residence, then just say good-bye to your hard-earned money.

Today I am here to explain how you can save lots of money by owning a home. Over the next 30 minutes, I'll be discussing three basic financial benefits of home ownership. What I say tonight could save you thousands of dollars over the next few years.

The next time you prepare your introduction, think about an effective rhetorical question you could use to capture and maintain your audience's attention.

Statistic

Another technique to use in an introduction is the statistic. Statistics are numerical data stated in a comprehensible manner for your audience. A speech to inform your audience about the successful three-part formula of *TV Guide* and *Reader's Digest*, delivered to a group of magazine distributors, could begin as follows:

> I'm delighted to speak with you today. As you know I'll be discussing the successful formula of two of the largest periodicals in the world, *Reader's Digest* and *TV Guide*.
>
> Most of us are familiar with these two giants of the publications industry, but we may be unaware of the extent of these industries. In 1995, *Reader's Digest* had a circulation of almost 18 million. And *TV Guide's* circulation was over 15 million.
>
> As magazine distributors, it's important for us to know our products fully so today I will explain the formula behind the successes of *TV Guide* and *Reader's Digest*.

Quotation

A quotation is a particularly effective way to inspire your audience and give some supplementary information on the content of your speech. In a speech before young businesspeople, your boss might want to quote Malcolm S. Forbes, founder of *Forbes* magazine and business executive extraordinaire. Here's an excerpt of a speech given to some business managers:

> One of America's leading entrepreneurs, the late Malcolm Forbes, founder of *Forbes* magazine and multimillionaire, once said, "Executives who get there and stay suggest solutions when they present problems."
>
> This afternoon I'm pleased to be talking with all of you aspiring managers. We'll be discussing the practical aspects of Forbes's quotation, learning in five simple steps how to become a problem solver.

You can select a quotation from someone famous, an expert in a particular area, or someone who has firsthand experience with a situation. Just make sure the quotation you use is meaningful in your speech and to your audience and that the person who is quoted has the authority, expertise, or experience to make the statement credible.

Story

Another effective way to engage your audience at the beginning of your speech is to tell a story. Let's say that your specific purpose is to persuade your audience (senior citizens who are prospective participants in your HMO, HEALTHCARE) about the benefits of membership. You could begin your speech in the following manner:

> Jane McDowell was an active and energetic 65-year-old woman. Last April she signed up for coverage in our senior citizen plan. She increased her coverage so that she would pay no deductible.
>
> In June of last year Jane fainted and was taken to the hospital. She spent two weeks in intensive care and was diagnosed with failure of the kidneys. Thanks to our HMO, Jane was able to receive a kidney transplant yesterday, her prognosis is excellent, and she never had to pay any additional money out of her own pocket.
>
> Today I'm pleased to be with you so that I can explain how HEALTH-CARE works and what benefits will be available to you.

People love to hear personal accounts or stories. A personal testimony or a narrative about someone else in your introduction can be both dramatic and engaging.

Once you've introduced your topic to your audience, turn your attention to the middle or body of your speech.

BODY

The body of your speech is also referred to as the middle, main section, or basic text of your speech. Here you will develop the main points of your speech. In the body, you will also elaborate on or expound upon these major themes of your talk.

When you organize the body of your speech, there are three surefire ways to do it right. The three most common and effective ways to organize your speech are according to topic, time, or problem-and-solution. We'll take a look at topical organization first.

Topical Organization

When you organize your body into topical units, you divide the main points into some common classification system. The topical organization is suitable for informative, persuasive, and entertaining speeches. An attractive aspect of the topical organization is that you can change the order of the main points depending upon the audience.

If your specific purpose is to persuade your audience of the two major benefits of the Boing garage spring, you could arrange the main points in the following ways:

Boing Garage Springs
Main Points in Topical Order
Example 1
I.   Boing springs are guaranteed for 100 years.
II.   Boing springs are the quietest springs available.
III. Boing springs are the cheapest springs available.

If, however, you are trying to sell Boing springs to some senior citizens, you may want to change the order of your main points. Because older customers may be on a tighter budget, your first point would emphasize the low cost.

Example 2
I.   Boing springs are the cheapest springs available.
II.   Boing springs are the quietest springs availbable.
III. Boing springs are guaranteed for 100 years.

Chronological Order

A second type of organizational structure to use in the body of your speech has to do with chronological order. Let's say that you have been asked to discuss the history of your small business's use of computers. The most effective way to organize your information would be according to time. Your main point outline might look like the following one:

My Use of Computers in My Small Business
Main Points Arranged in Chronological Order
I.   I assembled my first computer kit as a hobby in the 1950s.

II. The microprocessor had a huge impact on computer technology and my business.

III. I purchased my first low-cost, mass-marketed computer in the 1980s.

IV. My business computers today have more memory, storage, and computer power than ever before.

As you can see, the chronological pattern is ideal for handling historical matters.

Problem-and-Solution

A particularly effective organizational pattern to use in persuasive speaking is problem-and-solution. The first part, the problem or need section, emphasizes the necessity to change the way things are. The second component, the solution or satisfaction stage, has the resolution. If, for example, your specific purpose is to persuade your audience (city council) to ban skateboarding at the Marx Mall, you could use a problem-and-solution structure.

First, you would establish that there is a problem. You could point out that skateboarding has resulted in some serious accidents, loss of business, and destruction of property.

Second, in the solution portion of your speech, you would logically conclude that by banning skateboarding, there would be fewer accidents, more business, and less destruction of property. Your main points outline would appear as follows. Note also that the outline has been extended to include support for each main point. These subpoints are represented with capital letters.

It's Time To Ban Skateboarding at the Marx Mall
Main Points Outline—Problem-and-Solution Order
I. There is a serious problem with skateboarding at the Marx Mall.
   A. More than 50 accidents have occurred since people started skateboarding there five years ago.
   B. Research indicates that the 10% decrease in business over the past five years is due to skateboarding.
   C. Skateboarding mishaps have accounted for more than $2,000 in damaged property.
II. The solution to our problem is to ban skateboarding at the Marx Mall.
   A. Without skateboarding, there will be fewer accidents.

    B.   Our business will increase without skateboarding.

    C.   We will no longer have to pay for damaged property.

No matter what organizational structure you use, the important thing is that you are presenting your material as completely as possible in a coherent and clear fashion. The more organized your main points are, the better your audience will understand and remember what is said. Remember that organization in speaking, as well as in business, is a highly valued commodity.

CONCLUSION

Your conclusion summarizes what you've been saying in the body of your speech and leaves your audience with something dramatic and easily remembered. The ending is not the place to introduce any new concepts or facts, but rather the place to revisit the specific purpose or objective of your speech in a memorable fashion.

There are three simple and extremely popular ways to close your speech. These techniques include the use of repetition, the challenge, and the quotation. First, let's examine the use of repetition.

Repetition

Repetition of a message is one clear way to get an audience to remember what you've said. The next time you hear a commercial on television or the radio, listen to the number of times a name, phone number, or a two or three word concept is repeated. Contemplate the millions of dollars that advertisers pour into the research for production of those commercials! And then apply the use of repetition to your speeches.

Let's say that your boss has asked you to give a community public relations speech to your county's board of supervisors. Your specific purpose is to persuade your audience to participate in your company's annual fundraiser. Using repetition, your conclusion might sound something like this:

For all of the many reasons I have discussed over the past hour, please become part of our annual fundraiser. Remember how money from the fundraiser helped the little boy walk again. Remember how funds from last year's event enabled an inner city child to go to college. And remember how, because of the fundraiser, a new homeless shelter was built. Remember all these accom-

Quiz

1. Why is a specific purpose important in preparing your speech?
2. What are four techniques that you could use in your introduction?
3. Explain three ways to organize the main points in the body of your speech.
4. Define three techniques for concluding your speech.

Answer Key

1. A specific purpose helps you focus on exactly where your speech is headed. It will help you to organize your main points so that your audience will respond in a way that you intend them to.
2. The following four techniques are excellent devices to use in your introduction.
   a. Rhetorical Question
   b. Statistic
   c. Quotation
   d. Story
3. Three ways to organize the body of your speech include:
   a. Topical
   b. Chronological
   c. Problem-and-Solution
4. Three ways to conclude your speech include:
   a. Repetition
   b. Challenge
   c. Quotation

NEXT STEP

All right! You've done it again! Proceed ahead into Chapter 7, *Supporting Your Opinions.* Continue with your great work!

CHAPTER | 7

SUPPORTING YOUR OPINIONS

Most people have come away from a political speech, sales talk, or departmental report and thought, "It was an interesting speech, but somehow I'm just not convinced." Or perhaps you have been trying to persuade your supervisor that you really do need a raise and the boss just doesn't seem to be convinced. The problem in each example could be that you didn't employ enough supporting material to substantiate your opinions.

We've all experienced the *I think* phenomenon, where the speaker tries to persuade an audience in the following manner:

> As you know we're gathered here today to discuss the city council ordinance banning billboards in our city. Well, as you may know, I'm totally against this legislation. I think it's an outrage and totally unfair. I have lived in this city all my life, and I think this is the worst city council act I've ever seen. I think that we should think twice about reelecting our city officials. I think we're in for more problems if this ordinance passes.

Wouldn't you agree that this is not a convincing argument against the city council ordinance? In most situations, the *I think* statements don't hold a lot of water for anyone except the person who is stating them.

USING EVIDENCE

The positive alternative to *I think* declarations is to state your opinion and then support it with evidence. *Evidence* is proof that is helpful in leading your audience to your judgment. Let's replace the *I think* statements in the previous example with evidence.

> As you all know, I am strongly against city council ordinance #33343 to ban billboards in our city. I am against the ordinance for the following reasons:
> First, it is unfair and illegal to ban one type of advertising and not other types. The citizens of our community voted on Referendum #33393 that said we should allow billboards along with other types of advertising. Second, our city has already limited the number of billboards we can put up in this city. In addition, we have been most conservative in setting up the distances that billboards can be from our curbs, parks, and schools. No other city in the nation has such constraints.
> Third, if we outlaw billboards, we are setting ourselves up for a series of legal entanglements. Since we have already established legal billboard requirements, we would be in for court battles if we passed city council ordinance #33343. Therefore, I strongly object to city council ordinance #33343 and encourage all of you to fight its passage. Thank you.

The use of evidence in the second example contributes to a much stronger argument. There are five effective types of evidence that can be used in supporting your opinions: examples, quotations, statistics, definitions, and analogies. We'll begin with a discussion of examples.

Examples

An example is a story about a person or place that personalizes the point you are making. Many popular speakers, such as former President Reagan and bestselling author Norman Vincent Peale, frequently use anecdotes and examples as the best way to engage an audience and maintain their interest. While your example may

WORDS FROM THE WISE

"Before you try to convince anyone else be sure you are convinced, and if you cannot convince yourself, drop the subject."

—*John Patterson*

be hypothetical or true, research has demonstrated that audiences assign more credibility to factual examples.

Note in the following excerpt how an opinion is supported with an example. The assertion is that the company must provide a childcare facility to increase employee satisfaction.

> Briteco, our generally progressive company, needs to move into the 21st century in respect to parental benefits. It is imperative that we create a childcare facility for the hundreds of mothers who are our employees. These parents are forced to drive over 10 miles to place their babies in childcare.
>
> Many manufacturing plants like ours around the nation have instituted educational programs on site with overwhelmingly positive results. Capetowne, our major competitor, has had improved employee satisfaction ratings, fewer sick days reported, and more overtime clocked with less complaints from parents since their childcare facility was established.
>
> Imagine a factory where parents can visit their children at lunch and know that the company really cares about their welfare. Let's support our workers who are parents and keep up with the times.

Quotations

Another effective technique for reinforcing your opinions is to use a quotation. A quotation from an expert, a respected periodical, or someone who has firsthand experience is an excellent way to add weight to what you believe to be true. In the following excerpt, the assertion is that the purchase of teleconferencing equipment would be cost effective compared with the rental of such equipment.

> As most of you know, I think it is imperative we buy our own teleconferencing equipment. As Briteco's profits have steadily grown over the last two years, so

REMINDERS FOR USING EVIDENCE

1. Ask yourself if your evidence is accurate and current. For example, the population of Las Vegas increases by approximately 100,000 people each year, so keep your figures current.

2. Quote an expert or someone with relevant experience in a situation. Quoting a florist's opinion about television probably won't work at the National Broadcasters Convention.

3. Avoid lengthy quotations. Audiences want to develop eye contact, not watch you read. If you need a shorter quotation, paraphrase it.

4. Don't antagonize the audience with an overuse of statistics. A little statistical analysis goes a long way.

5. Always round off your statistics. Could you remember that 589,932 people live in Tucson, Arizona? However, you could remember that 600,000 people live in Tucson.

6. Explain what the statistics mean to your audience. Knowing that one out of four small business owners in your audience will probably qualify for a SBA loan is more meaningful than saying that one million small business owners in the community will qualify.

7. Define a complex or technical word the first time you use it. The same rule applies for acronyms. Don't give your audience a chance to feel perplexed.

---

has our use of teleconferencing. Our marketing plans indicate that we will continue to increase our teleconferencing efforts over the next ten years.

Briteco Teleconferencing Manager Andrew Boyd states, "It would be cost effective to purchase teleconferencing rather than to continue to lease it." Boyd suggests that if we make this expenditure this year "we will save over $20,000 over the next five years."

On the basis of Boyd's recommendation and the success that our competitors have experienced with leased teleconferencing equipment, I strongly encourage us to make this purchase.

Statistics

Statistics relate a fact in numerical description. Any fact that can be quantified is particularly attractive in business. In fact, statistical information provides the substance of most oral and written business reports. So, if you can incorporate statistics into your supporting materials, you'll be one step ahead of the game. In the following excerpt, the assertion is that the number of telecommuters has increased over the past three years.

> There has been a dramatic increase in the number of people in business who work at home. The number of telecommuters—company employees who work from home part-time or full-time during normal business hours—increased by almost two million over the last three years. This is an 18% annual growth rate. Telecommuter experts project that this trend will continue well into the next century.

While statistics can be very persuasive, you should avoid using too many of them or too much detail. Your audience will retain your statistics much better if you round off your numbers and use visual aids for statistical information.

Definitions

Definitions provide meaning and clarification of unfamiliar or ambiguous words. If you are speaking to a group that may not be familiar with the word entrepreneur, you could provide the following definition.

> The word *entrepreneur* is derived from a French word that means to undertake. In America, an entrepreneur is a risk-taker who organizes, operates, and assumes the risk for a business venture.

In addition to defining words and concepts, you also need to explain what acronyms represent. While you may know that a CD stands for both a compact disc and a certificate of deposit, not everyone may have the same understanding. You also need to use definitions when referring to foreign words or jargon used in your business or industry. One of your responsibilities as a speaker is to make things easy to understand. Always remember that a puzzled audience is turned off by things they don't comprehend.

Analogies

While analogies can be both literal and figurative, business speakers rely primarily on the literal comparison. Literal analogies are used in reports and end-of-the-year summaries to compare earnings per share or percentages of increase over the last year. In business, there is great value in creating clear, succinct numerical analogies.

Figurative analogies make a comparison between the unknown (for example, the workings of a microprocessor) and the known (the way a brain functions). Figurative analogies are particularly effective when explaining a very complex concept or operation. The key to effective analogies is to create a comparison that the audience understands. Working from a familiar concept, audiences will more easily grasp the new idea.

Form the habit of supporting your opinions with examples, quotations, statistics, definitions, and analogies. Not only will your audience find your material more credible, but you will also notice an improvement in your writing and your ability to make rational decisions in business.

GATHERING INFORMATION

Now that we've established the importance of using evidence, let's consider some important aspects of gathering your evidence. For most of the talks you deliver, the information you need is probably in your head or in records that you can easily access. The data you need may be in unpublished business minutes, reports, questionnaires, journals, or letters. If, however, the information you need is not readily available, you could rely upon a few of the following tried-and-true ways of finding evidence.

Surveys

An excellent way to gather comprehensive information about ideas or situations is to conduct a survey. If you want to demonstrate that employee satisfaction is at an all-time high, then perhaps administering a survey would help you to find out. You would be able to use the firsthand results to support your assertion that things are going well.

In the same way, if you suspect that customer representatives at your automobile service garage could be more amiable when processing information, you could give customers a satisfaction card to fill out. Then you could use the information to ascertain whether customer service was all that it should be. Finally, you could use your data as evidence in your speech.

Perhaps your business needs to know if there really does need to be additional space in the parking lot. By monitoring the lot over a week's period, you could determine if new construction was necessary.

Surveys can be as simple or as involved as you need them to be. The positive aspect of surveys lies in your direct participation in their design and administration.

Interviews

An interview is a formal two-person conversation with a predetermined purpose. Let's say that you have been asked to give a short biographical speech about the president of your labor union at the next regional conference. When the information you have about the president isn't enough, you decide that a telephone interview would provide the essentials you're looking for. In consideration of everyone's best interests, you need to incorporate the following recommendations into your interviewing techniques.

Interviewing Tips

First, determine your purpose or goal. Are you trying to find out background information about the person or his motivations for success? Is there a fact you need to check or is your objective to secure a catchy quotation? Because it is important that you spend your time in a productive manner, you'll need to plan ahead and know what you want as a result of the interview. At the beginning of your interview, make sure to share your purpose with the respondent. Then you'll both be focused.

Part of your preparation will also be to know as much as you can about the person you are interviewing and his or her business. Read resumes, booklets, annual reports, or anything that will update you on current information. Your knowledge will increase your credibility with your interviewee, and at the same time increase your confidence.

Second, you'll need to plan out questions you want to ask. Your questions should be clear and sincere. A question such as, "Do you consider the morale of our employees good, great, or better than average?" is difficult, if not impossible, to answer since the preceding adjectives are so relative.

Questions should also be open-ended instead of closed. An open-ended question introduces a subject, giving a respondent a great deal of freedom in answering. A closed question guides the response much more. An open-ended question would ask, "Would you explain the advantages to employees of owning a 401(k) plan?" A closed question would be one such as, "Do you agree that owning a 401(k) plan is in the best interest of your employees?" Notice that the closed questions require a short, one- or two-word response, shutting off any additional ideas your interviewee may have.

You can also use probing questions to delve deeper into issues or concepts that a respondent may not have adequately covered. For instance, you can always follow up an inadequate response with, "Can you give me an example to explain that

REMINDERS FOR INTERVIEWING

1. Determine your purpose for conducting the interview.
2. Prepare for the interview.
3. Write out your questions.
4. Use open-ended questions.
5. Listen carefully to the interviewee.
6. Practice courtesy and consideration before, during, and after the interview.

concept?" or "How would a plant supervisor apply your strategies for success?" Probing questions will help to clarify the responses and assist you in getting to the heart of each issue.

If you find that your respondent is becoming too vague or confused in his or her answers, you could use a mirror question. This is a question that restates what has already been said. For example, "Do I understand you correctly when you say that there are three major career tracks that a cashier can take to become a manager?" or "Do you mean that your brokers will have only limited access to Network A?" Mirror questions can provide clarification that may be extremely important when you begin to incorporate this evidence into your speech.

A third consideration in conducting an interview is to listen. Sounds easy, but in actuality listening is a difficult skill that most people take for granted. Give your interviewee a chance to respond to your questions; no matter how tempting it might be to interrupt and state your mind, don't do it. You already know what *you* think. You need to be concerned about gaining information from someone else.

Finally, make sure that you are considerate and courteous before, during, and after an interview. Thank your respondent verbally and also with a thank-you note after the interview. Kindness pays off and you should treat people the way that you would want to be treated.

REFERENCE MATERIALS

When you don't have the information you need right at your fingertips, you may want to explore a library near you. Most libraries have extensive business sections where great sources of both general and specific information are held. There are encyclopedias of business and marketing that provide an overview of almost any topic in those areas. And there are books like *Standard and Poor's Register of Cor-*

REMINDERS FOR GATHERING EVIDENCE

1. Rely on documents at work as support in your speeches. Minutes, reports, memoranda, and other written pieces in your business can be used to support your claims.

2. Surveys are an excellent firsthand method of collecting data to support your points. You can control both the structure and the administration of surveys.

3. If you don't already have them, purchase a complete dictionary and a thesaurus. They're indispensable when you're working on a presentation.

4. Keep track of where you found your evidence. You or someone in your audience may want to find the information again.

5. When searching for information, always consider the purpose of your speech and the audience you'll be addressing. Make every attempt to find and state evidence that will relate to your purpose and be meaningful to your audience.

porations, Directors, and Executives that list the names, addresses, executives, and sales figures for over 50,000 corporations.

Most states have their own directories for businesses, and there are numerous compilations of sales, manufacturing, and services aids. There is even a *Million Dollar Directory* that will keep you abreast of million-dollar companies. The sources of business information are endless, so you will probably want to secure the assistance of a reference librarian to help narrow your search.

There may be times when you want some statistical information. Books like *Statistical Abstracts of the United States* will provide a broad spectrum of numerical facts about national and international businesses and consumer purchasing patterns, as well as as wealth of demographic information. *Consumer Resource Handbook* lists the tips on buying products and the New York Stock Exchange will furnish you with the essential facts on the stock market.

Other valuable books include the *National Directory*, which lists the names, addresses, and phone numbers of businesses, nonprofit associations, and governmental agencies. *Webster's College Thesaurus* will give you synonyms (words that mean the same thing) and antonyms (words that have an opposite meaning). And *Simpson's Contemporary Quotations* may provide just the quotation you need to end your speech.

Libraries have business sections where you can find the most current books, magazines, and newspapers. *Forbes, Inc., Money, Wall Street Journal,* and *Working Woman* are just a few of the thousands of publications that cover all aspects of business.

Most libraries will have computers and electronic software that simplify the process of finding evidence. You can type in a subject, name, or title and retrieve citations (the title, date, and publication info) for numerous articles. If this type of search seems unmanageable to you, there are always reference librarians to help you find your materials. Don't be afraid to ask for help.

With so many reference materials available today, there should be no problem in finding evidence for your talks. Visit the business section of the library and find out where things are located before you need your evidence. Becoming familiar with the reference materials in the library now will save you some time when you need to use them later.

Keeping Track of Your Sources

Whether you are finding information for a presentation or for another purpose, it's a good idea to make a habit of writing down where you found your information. This means recording the name of the book or magazine, author, date, and page numbers where you found your information.

There are two reasons for recording your sources. First, if you ever need to take another look at the material, you'll know where to go. And second, if after your speech, anyone questions where you found your evidence, you'll have the information at your fingertips. You can increase your credibility by always being prepared.

Apply your new skills in the following exercises, and then complete the questions.

EXERCISES

A. Prepare and present a five-minute speech to inform your audience about your business's performance last year. Base the evidence in your speech on an annual report or other publications from work. Use a topical structure with three main points to organize your speech and compose an introduction and conclusion that incorporate quotations or statistics. Practice your speech and deliver it to someone or tape it. Get feedback from your audience.

B. Browse through the reference materials in the business section of your library. Find one meaningful quotation, statistic, and example that you could use in a future speech. Use the computer for locating materials on businesses that are your competition.

C. Interview someone in a professional position that you would like to have 10 years from now. Prepare for your interview and remember to ask open-ended questions and to listen. Then, based on your interview, list at least five main points of the interview.

Quiz

1. Discuss five types of evidence that you could use in your speeches.
2. Explain three sources for gathering your evidence.
3. Why is it important to focus on your purpose and audience when gathering information?

Answer Key

1. Five types of evidence you can use in your speeches include:
   a. Examples
   b. Quotations
   c. Statistics
   d. Definitions
   e. Analogies
2. Three ways to gather evidence for your speech include:
   a. Surveys
   b. Interviews
   c. Reference materials
3. By focusing on your purpose and audience, you will find evidence that is both relevant to your specific purpose and meaningful to your audience. Since there is so much supporting material available to us, we need to narrow our search based on our purpose and audience.

NEXT STEP

Congratulations on completing another chapter! You're doing great. Proceed and keep up the good work in Chapter 8, *Being Aware of Language.*

CHAPTER | 8

BEING AWARE OF LANGUAGE

Most successful businesspeople agree that communicating is a reciprocal process. It involves the exchange of information, both the sending and receiving of a message. As a speaker, you must try to use the most accurate, complete, and clear words so that your audience will decipher the message you intend them to.

FOCUS ON YOUR AUDIENCE

There are many ways that you can focus on the members of your audience. One practical aspect of using language involves the replacement of *I*, *we*, and *our* with *you*. Examine the following examples.

Rather than say:
I have evaluated this project and come to the conclusion that the recommendations are excellent.

Say:

Your recommendations on this project are excellent.

Rather than say:

We are very appreciative of the fine job on the west wing.

Say:

You did an excellent job on the west wing.

Recognize that your task is to make your presentation as relevant and meaningful to your audience as you can. By stating sentences in a *you* construction, your audience will view themselves as the top priority and see the benefits of your presentation clearly.

MISCOMMUNICATION

Miscommunication in business can occur when people are imprecise, inaccurate, and inconsiderate in using the English language. Note how clarification of the way you say something can make a major difference in meaning.

Many people in this room will be able to afford the huge amount of money that an average house costs today.

versus

Approximately one out of four people in this room will be able to afford the $110,000 necessary to purchase a home today.

Let me explain how to use the equipment. First, you'll need to take all of the paper and place it in there.

versus

Let me explain how to use the HP 232 laser printer. First, you'll need to bring four pounds of 8 1/2 by 11 inch paper and place it on the white file cabinet next to the Cane printer.

Then make sure everything is ready for the visit.

versus

Then you'll need to place a report, water glass, pen, and notebook on the table in front of each chair. Also make sure that there are two pitchers of water on each of the three tables.

As you can see, being specific in your use of language can ultimately prevent a problem from occurring. Let's take a look at several other ways we can use our language more effectively.

DEFINE RELATIVE WORDS

A study in a psychology journal found that words with relative meaning need to be explained to be correctly understood. For example, when stating "It's going to take a really long time to complete this project," your audience could infer that you mean two months or five years. It would be better to say, "It's going to take at least four months to complete this project." Or instead of noting, "We are projecting a large crowd for the sale," you should state, "Our company is projecting a crowd of approximately 4,000 people for the sale."

Remember that any time you use a relative word, you'll need to explain its meaning. Once you get into the practice of defining your terms, you'll narrow your audience's interpretation and limit any confusion that could occur.

USE CONCRETE WORDS

Another habit to practice is to focus on the use of concrete rather than abstract words. Concrete words are more specific, whereas abstract words are more general. While concrete words conjure up an image that you can visualize in your mind, abstract words are more ambiguous and can have several interpretations. As a rule, concrete language is preferred in business. The following examples replace abstract words with the favored, concrete words.

Abstract:
The first thing is to remove the computers from room 16.

Concrete:
The first condition of our contract is to remove the computers from room 16.

Abstract:
Investigation of the case suggests that Ms. Right was wrong.

Concrete:
I think that Ms. Right was wrong.

Abstract:
They decided that we should receive $20,000 for our marketing campaign.

Concrete:
The Board of Directors decided that our Purchasing Department should receive $20,000 for our marketing campaign.

Abstract:
We visited the tall building there.

Concrete:
We visited the Sears Tower, the tallest building in Chicago.

When you use concrete language, your audience will have a clearer mental picture of the message you are trying to convey. So use concrete language and take one more step toward becoming the speaker you've always wanted to be.

AVOID WORDINESS

In business, time is money, so try to save both time and money by creating a concise message. One way to do this is by deleting words that you don't need. For instance, rather than state "At this point in time," just say "Now." Or, rather than say, "During the time that," use "While." The following list may help you to avoid wordiness.

Instead of:
In the city of Tucson...

Say:
In Tucson...

Instead of:
The reason is because...

Say:
Because...

Instead of:
During the course of your...

Say:
During...

Instead of:
Personal friend...

Say:
Friend...

Instead of:
In point of fact...

Say:
In fact...

Instead of:
By the same token...

Say:
Also...

Instead of:
By virtue of the fact that...

Say:
Because...

Instead of:
At an early date...

Say:
Soon...

It's also important to delete the following phrases and sentence from your speeches:

To tell you the truth...

and so on and so forth...

If I knew more about this topic, I could probably explain it better.

EXPLAIN JARGON

No matter what business you're in, there will be some specialized language or jargon that only your trade or profession uses. If your audience is unfamiliar with the jargon you use, you can confuse and alienate them. Therefore, always explain jargon as well as any other foreign, complex, or unfamiliar words.

For example, when using jargon such as, "We must begin a needs assessment of the decrease in home lending applications," consider whether your audience knows what you mean. It may be in the best interest of your audience to say, "We should find out why fewer people are applying for home loans." And of course, if you don't understand the language, don't ever present the material to your audience.

DEFINE ACRONYMS

Acronyms are words formed from the initial letters of a name. The New York Stock Exchange becomes the acronym NYSE and the Friends of Sabino Canyon is referred to as FOSC. But unless you're using these terms in a sentence, you may not know that. So define your acronyms when you use them.

As a speaker, it's imperative to define your acronym when it is used for the first time. And, if the acronym is more that four words long, you may want to define it a second time for your audience. Never assume that your audience does not need a definition of your acronym. Get into the habit of explaining each acronym and avoid confronting the quizzical glances of your audience.

POWERFUL LANGUAGE

Many studies focus on the use of powerful language. Researchers study what words people use when they speak and the effect that language has on the speaker's image. Powerful language is interpreted as persuasive and believable, resulting in a credible and positive image for the speaker. Nonpowerful language is interpreted as less credible, creating a negative image of the speaker. Nonpowerful language is most easily observable in four categories: tag questions, disclaimers, hedges, and hesitations. Let's begin with a discussion of tag questions.

Tag Questions

Tag questions are asked after a statement is made. The tag question diminishes the forcefulness of the statement, so speakers are considered to be less credible if they use them a lot. Examples of tag questions would be the following: "It's about time that we accepted the policy, don't you agree?" or, "We'd better change advertising companies, don't you think?" By limiting the number of tag questions you use, you'll increase the powerfulness of your speech.

Disclaimers

Disclaimers are words preceding a second set of words that limit the meaning of the latter. Some frequently used disclaimers include phrases such as the following: "I'm not really sure about this, but…," "This answer is probably all wrong, but…," and "Everyone knows more about this than me, so…." As you can see, disclaimers are words the speaker uses that "put down" their own credibility. This remark also decreases the speaker's influence in the eyes of the audience. Being aware of what you say and changing words that negatively affect your image will help you to become a more powerful speaker.

Hedges

Hedges are a group of words that seem to circumvent an issue or an opinion. For example, rather than say, "I'm kinda unhappy about this situation," you should be more direct and say, "I'm unhappy about this situation." Or instead of saying, "I guess I'd like to begin this campaign," deal with an issue directly by stating, "I'd like to begin this campaign." As you can see in the previous examples, hedges are imprecise and are used to skirt an issue. Audiences tend to label a speaker who uses an excessive amount of hedges as less believable and less credible. For more powerful language, watch your use of hedges.

Hesitations

Hesitations occur when a speaker is unsure of his or her position and pauses or interjects unrelated words. Because it's important in business to be assertive and forthright, you need to eliminate hesitations to speak confidently and immediately. Examine the following common hesitations and the preferred way to phrase each statement:

Hesitation:
Ah, can I have only a few minutes of your time?

Correction:
May I speak with you?

Hesitation:
Well, you see, I was wondering…er…if we could try this plan?

Correction:
Could we try this plan?

Hesitation:
I wanted to tell you…ah…if you can, could you be on time?

Correction:
Please be on time.

The first step in using powerful language is to become aware of the words you use. If you do note a pattern in the use of tag questions, disclaimers, hedges, and hesitations, then work on eliminating them. Remember that speech habits, like most other habits, take time and perseverance to change. Just decide that you will increase the power of your language and you will succeed!

CONNECTIVES

Have you ever been in a business meeting or attended a speech and found that your mind started to wander? And then, when you focused back on the speech, you were confused about where the speaker was headed? Research has demonstrated that audience distraction is a common occurrence. In fact, some studies say that people "tune out" several times during a presentation.

As speakers, it is our responsibility to keep our audience on target so that they will understand and retain as much of our material as possible. One of the techniques that we can use is to incorporate connectives into our speech. *Connectives* are words, phrases, or sentences that bridge or attach two distinct ideas or thoughts.

Let's say that you have been asked to explain to a new group of employees how to get the most from a defined-benefit plan. You've organized your material into five basic steps. When you deliver your speech, plan to designate each of the five steps with a connective such as *First...*, *Second...*, *Third...*, *Next...*, and *Finally....* Other connectives to use in this situation would be *Lastly...*, *The most important step...*, and *Consider this fourth point.* The bottom line is that these connectives will keep you and your audience in the same place.

When you're establishing a cause-and-effect relationship in your speech, you can use connectives such as *As a result, Consequently*, and *Therefore.* For example, if you're establishing the connection between courteous telephone skills and repeat business, you could incorporate the following connective in your statement. "As a result of your superior and courteous telephone skills, our repeat business has remained at approximately 80%." Cause and effect connectives assist your audience to stay involved in where you're headed.

It's also important to designate the conclusion of your speech. Rather than end your talk with "I'm done" or "That's it," you could say "Finally...," "Let me restate the three major points of my speech," or, "Now that I've almost concluded my speech...." Because your audience is more likely to recall what you said first and last in your speech, make sure they know you're about to conclude your speech.

There's a common adage in speechmaking that says, "Tell your audience where you're going, where you are, and where you've been." Longer connectives that provide previews and reviews of your material can assist you in accomplishing this goal. A preview would be something like the following:

In the last portion of my speech today, I will define what mutual funds are, introduce you to the five most popular funds, and then explain how to find a fund that's just right for you. Let's begin with a definition of a mutual fund...

An example of a review would be something like the following:

Now that I've explained how straight-life, joint-and-survivor, and life annuities work, you should be able to determine which is best for you.

The following list of connectives can also be used to bridge two ideas together.

I've saved the most important point for last…

Let's examine the worst part of the plan…

What should this mean to you?

So remember these three points…

The answer? Let me explain…

The bottom line is that connectives help to keep your audience involved and on track. Try to incorporate them into your speeches so that your audience will receive the exact message you are trying to convey. As we know, the key to a successful speech is what the audience receives, not what we intend them to receive.

SUBSTANDARD LANGUAGE

There are almost a million words in the English language. In fact, English is considered to have the largest vocabulary on earth. Not every word that people say is acceptable or standard English. Many words that are used each day are substandard and unacceptable, particularly in business. The following list covers some substandard language and the accepted version.

Rather than:	Say:
ain't	isn't or aren't
nohow	anyway
This here is new.	This is new.
I am plenty hungry.	I am hungry.
It's for him and I.	It's for him and me.
Anyways, I knew that.	Anyway, I knew that.
She seen it.	She saw it.
He done it.	He did it.
can't hardly	can hardly
in regards to	regarding
Irregardless…	Regardless…

A and An

An is placed before words that begin with *a, e, i, o, u,* and sometimes *h. A* is used with the other 19 letters of the alphabet. Look over the following uses of *an* and *a.*

Incorrect:	Correct:
I saw a auditor.	I saw an auditor.
I picked up a envelope.	I picked up an envelope.
That is a understatement.	That is an understatement.
It was a historic moment.	It was an historic moment.

COMMON MISUSES

Four common misuses of words in the English language include eager/anxious, can/may, affect/effect, and further/farther. Read through the following examples.

Eager/Anxious

An *eager* employee feels excited at the prospect of taking on more responsibilities. An *anxious* employee is worried about additional tasks.

Can/May

Can denotes an ability to do something, whereas *may* involves gaining permission. At a business luncheon, you would politely ask your colleague, "May I please have the salt?" However, it is correct to say, "You can type 30 words per minute." Use *can* when determining whether someone has the competence to perform a task and *may* when requesting permission to do something.

Affect/Effect

These two words sound very much alike, but there are differences in their meanings. *Affect* is a verb that means "to influence." *Effect* is generally a noun that means "result." Use these words in the following manner:

The sale affects the overall profit.

How will the change affect business?

The effect of the sale is seen in the profits.

What effect will the change have on business?

Less commonly, *effect* is a verb that means, "to bring about."

Because of our situation, the general *effected* our retreat.

Further/Farther

Farther is always used when you are talking about a distance. *Further* refers to a quantity or degree. Examine the examples that follow:

Is Santa Fe or Houston farther?

This issue needs further investigation.

PRONUNCIATION

There's nothing worse than when a speaker says, "I really don't know how to pronounce this word," and then proceeds to prove herself correct. As a member of the audience you think, "Why didn't she prepare? She knew she was going to deliver this speech."

Unless you are asked to deliver an impromptu speech, there's no excuse for not looking up the word in a dictionary. Dictionaries list words with their phonetic pronunciation in parentheses. A phonetic guide in the front of the dictionary will assist you in sounding out a word. And if there are two phonetic spellings, use the first because it is the preferred pronunciation. The following lists contain words that are commonly mispronounced. Beside each word is the accepted pronunciation:

Word:	Mispronunciation:	Correct form:
idea	i-de-r	i-de-a
ask	axe	ask
often	off-ten	off-en
library	li-bare-e	li-brar-e
drowned	drown-did	drownd
going	gon-na	go-ng
pen	pin	pen
introduce	in-ter-dus	in-tro-dus
probably	prob-ble	pro-ba-ble

WORDS FROM THE WISE

"Language is not only the vehicle of thought; it is the great and efficient instrument in thinking."

—*Sir H. Davy*

It's also important to enunciate each word. Rather than blend syllables together as in, "Whachagonnadoaboutit?" you should say, "What are you going to do about it?" Enunciation and standard English are imperative in business.

NONFLUENCIES

It's quite natural for speakers to include an occasional *um*, *ah*, or *er* in their speech. However, when these nonfluencies, as they are referred to, interfere with the content of a speech, then a speaker needs to concentrate on eliminating them.

Tape your next speech or have a friend tabulate the number of times you use nonfluencies. If the number exceeds 20 nonfluencies in a five-minute period, then it will be in your best interest to reduce that number. Most people eliminate their use of nonfluencies by pausing a second or two before they speak. The problem should clear up if you take your time and concentrate on what you are going to say.

NONDISCRIMINATORY LANGUAGE

In business, you must make sure to use nondiscriminatory language. Discriminatory language forms stereotypes of people according to gender, ethnic group, or physical handicap. Study the following lists of nondiscriminatory tips.

Nondiscriminatory Tips

1. Avoid exclusive use of male pronouns (he, his, or him) if you are unsure of the gender of your subject. Rather than always using male pronouns in sentences, remain neutral or use both male and female pronouns. Examine the following corrections:

Rather than say:
Everyone will receive his bonus check.

Say:
Everyone will receive his or her bonus check.

Rather than say:
He was wondering about his job.

Say:
The employee was wondering about jobs.

2. Avoid the use of *-man* on the end of some compound words.

Instead of saying:	Say:
postman	postal carrier
businessman	businessperson
chairman	chairperson
salesman	salesperson

3. Use *Mr.* and *Ms.* as titles for men and women in business. Both men and women should be addressed by *Dr.* or *Professor* if they have acquired an advanced degree.

4. Make sure that you have used parallel terms for men and women.

Rather than say:
man and wife

Say:
husband and wife

Rather than say:
As a female CEO, she

Say:
As a CEO, she

WORDS FROM THE WISE

"When I was a child and studied about the Pilgrim Fathers I supposed they were all bachelors, as I never found a word about their wives."

—*Ella S. Stewart*

"Words like *spinster* and *old maid* as opposed to *bachelor* and *playboy* illustrate how we view women who do not choose to marry or who miss out on the chance if they want it."

—*Charlotte Holt Clinebell*

"If a woman is swept off a ship into the water, the cry is 'Man overboard!' If she is killed by a hit-and-run driver, the charge is 'manslaughter.' If she is injured on the job, the coverage is 'workmen's compensation.' But if she arrives at a threshold marked 'Men Only,' she knows the admonition is not intended to bar animals or plants or inanimate objects. It is meant for her."

—*Alma Graham*

Rather than say:
men and girls

Say:
men and women

5. Avoid condescending words such as *chick, babe, hon,* or *sweetie.*

6. Make substitutes for sexist verbs.

Rather than say:
She will man the phones.

Say:
She will operate the phones.

Being aware of the language you use and correcting any discriminatory language is imperative in any business. Fair treatment of all of your customers, regardless of gender, age, or race, will guarantee more satisfied customers.

REMINDERS FOR LANGUAGE

1. Focus on your audience, not yourself.
2. Achieve clarity by being concrete.
3. Avoid wordiness. Be succinct.
4. Explain acronyms.
5. Practice correct pronunciations. Use your dictionary.
6. Choose nondiscriminatory language.

Please review some of the major points of this chapter by reading the following list of reminders and completing the exercises and questions.

EXERCISES

A. Find five unfamiliar words in a newspaper or magazine. Define and pronounce each word according to the information you find in a dictionary.

B. Analyze the language use of a friend or coworker. Evaluate the language according to wordiness, concreteness, powerful words, and discriminatory language. Ask a friend or relative to analyze your use of language.

Quiz

1. Choose *a* or *an* in the following examples.

_____ envelope   _____ looseleaf notebook

_____ briefcase   _____ orange file

_____ hardcover   _____ yellow eraser

2. What can you do to avoid discriminatory language?

3. What are four ways to make your language clearer?

Answer Key

1. an envelope   a looseleaf notebook

   a briefcase   an orange file

   a hardcover   a yellow eraser

2. Avoid the exclusive use of male pronouns and the suffix *-man*; use parallel terms, and *Mr.* and *Ms.* in business.

3. Define relative words, jargon, and acronyms. Use connectives and eliminate substandard English.

NEXT STEP

Congratulations for completing another chapter! Way to go! Continue your journey to better speaking by reading the next chapter, *Delivering Your Presentation In Style.*

CHAPTER | 9

DELIVERING YOUR PRESENTATION IN STYLE

There's one rule in speaking that you must never forget: One cannot *not* communicate. This seemingly simple sentence is actually quite profound. What it means is that whether or not your intention is to send a message to someone, you are still always communicating something to someone.

If during a presentation, you are jingling the coins in your pockets, an audience may construe that you are nervous. Or if you're constantly looking at the ceiling, they may think you're not interested in them. And if, heaven forbid, you are playing with your hair, an audience may deduce that you're not serious about your material.

Since the success of your presentation is determined by the response of your audience, you must always be aware of the way you come across to others. This means that you need to examine your body language as well as your verbal delivery.

Fortunately, there are tried and true methods for relating well to others. By applying the latest research to how you act and speak, anyone can improve his or her delivery skills.

Let's begin our study by examining body language, or what some behavioral scientists refer to as nonverbal communication. Then, later in the chapter, we'll discuss verbal delivery.

BODY LANGUAGE

Nonverbal communication or body language is important in business. When you smile, customers think you care about them. If you are slouched over and dressed in dirty, smelly clothes, then an audience may construe that you're a slob with no confidence.

Researchers indicate that 65% of the emotional meaning of a message comes from the nonverbal delivery. Furthermore studies indicate that people who are skilled in nonverbal communication (facial expressions, movement, physical appearance, and gestures) are perceived as more interesting, more intelligent, and more likable than people in the study who do not have effective nonverbal skills.

In order to become more effective in nonverbal delivery, we'll examine five essential areas in body language. These include posture, facial expression, clothing, gestures, and proximity to your audience. We'll begin with posture.

Posture

Good posture is important for several reasons. First, a relaxed yet erect posture can contribute to boosting a speaker's confidence. Speakers look and feel more confident when they stand up straight. Second, good posture improves the quality of your voice. And finally, your self-assured posture sets the tone for your audience. If your posture is too stiff, then listeners may feel uncomfortable. If you're slouched or in a semi-sleep position, they may feel inattentive.

The key of good posture is equally distributing your weight on both feet, which are shoulder-width apart. Shoulders are back and the chin is up. It's also better to place the majority of your weight on the balls, rather than the heels, of your feet. And remember to relax!

Facial Expression

Eye contact is a key component of facial expression. You need to look at as many members of your audience as you can. It's important not to favor a few special people in the audience but rather to rotate your eye contact to various sections of

WORDS FROM THE WISE

"What flowers are to nature, smiles are to humanity. They are but trifles, to be sure, but, scattered along life's pathway, the good they do is inconceivable."

—*Joseph Addison*

your audience. Start in the front, then the right side, the back, and then the left side. Good eye contact means connecting with as many people as you can in the most natural manner that you're capable of.

It is of primary importance that every member of your audience feels that you are talking to that individual personally. And you cannot accomplish this task if you are scanning the wall, staring at the ceiling, or glued to your notes.

Another crucial part of facial expression has to do with the emotions we convey. Studies indicate that smiling creates a favorable impression, that CEOs smile more than other workers, and that smiling can actually make you feel better. Of course, smiling is not appropriate if you're discussing the down trend in sales or the multiple layoffs at your factory, but for most occasions, optimism pays off and is contagious.

You can also use your face to express a variety of other emotions. Raise your eyebrows to express skepticism or curiosity, and squint your eyes to demonstrate anger. Do whatever it takes to dramatize and reinforce the emotional aspect of your presentations.

Clothing

The clothing we wear to work says something about us, even if we don't give our dress much thought. Research tells us that people are more inclined to obey a well-dressed person than one in lower-status clothing. When it comes to business attire, the following three rules ring loud and clear.

First, dress appropriately for your position. Your clothes must be suitable for your workplace. Notice what your boss and other managers are wearing. Then select your own clothing to coordinate with their look. Many image consultants agree that instead of dressing for your current position, you should dress for the job that is one step up from yours. In addition to looking good for your clients and colleagues, dressing well does a great deal for one's self-esteem.

Always dress in comfortable clothing. There's nothing worse than a jacket or pants that are a bit snug or a skirt that barely zips. If sitting causes your dress to hike up, then wear something that's more comfortable.

It's also best to dress conservatively in business. Unless you're working on Melrose Place, "sexy" is best left for your after-hours wardrobe. It's a waste of your time and your business's money to be at work stressed by the uncomfortable fit of your outfit. Therefore, the best rule is to be comfortable, conservative, and carefree in your dress.

Cleanliness is next to godliness in most business environments where sanitary conditions and clean clothes are imperative. Get in the habit of dry-cleaning or washing your clothes on a regular basis. And when you live in a highly populated area and are dealing with hundreds of people on a daily basis, wash your hands every chance you get.

Gestures and Movement

There are basically three important points to remember when using gestures. First, your movements have to look absolutely natural. In fact, the more natural you appear, the more likely you'll be able to connect with your audience.

Second, both your movement and gestures need to coincide with what you are saying. If you're discussing the three main reasons to support your proposal, then you could use one, two, and then three fingers to emphasize your point. When you discuss the size of the new ultra-lightweight laptops, you could show your audience. And when you are discussing the major reason why people are insecure, you could lean or walk toward your audience.

When you speak, practice shrugging your shoulders when you don't understand, shaking your head up, and making an O.K. sign with your hand. If it feels natural, try to incorporate these and other gestures into your speech.

WORDS FROM THE WISE

"Clothes don't make the man, but good clothes have got many a man a good job."

—*Thomas Fuller*

"Dress does not make a man, but it often makes a successful one."

—*Disraeli*

REMINDERS FOR USING GESTURES AND MOVEMENT

1. Always appear natural in your use of gestures and movement.
2. Coordinate your gestures and movements with what you say.
3. Too many gestures and too much movement are worse than none.

If you're a person who never gestures, at first add one or two subtle gestures when you talk and then gradually increase that number. Gestures will make you seem more interesting, as well as emphasize important points.

Third, remember that there is something a lot worse than not using any gestures, and that is using too many gestures. Gestures are most effective when they are so natural that an audience will look at your presentation in totality, instead of thinking about your overuse of arm, hand, or body movements. When you are racing around the stage or waving your arms neurotically at a meeting, the end result may be a frenzied audience instead of a well-informed, persuaded, or entertained group of people.

It's also very important to avoid distracting mannerisms. Never twist a paper clip, chew on a pencil, twist your hair, or scratch your back. These movements just get in the way of an effective presentation. Remember that you're a professional and you need to act accordingly.

Keep an eye on people whom you admire. Observe their use of gestures and try to incorporate the ones that would work for you.

Proximity to Your Audience

When you are using gestures or movement in your speech, respect audience members' space. Each of us has our own territory and we begin to feel a little nervous if someone gets in our space. Most people have a personal distance of approximately one arm's length before they feel uneasy. This is one of the reasons people become a bit unnerved when they stand next to strangers in an elevator. Be aware whenever you interact with someone that you shouldn't cross personal space boundaries.

THE IMPORTANCE OF YOUR VOICE

Many times how you say something may be just as important as what you say. Think about the last time someone told you that everything was all right, but the

WORDS FROM THE WISE

"What you say and what you do must be one."

—*Chiang Kai-Shek*

"There is no index of character so sure as the voice."

—*Disraeli*

speaker's voice indicated something else. Your voice can convey a powerful message, regardless of your intent.

Studies indicate that certain vocal qualities are most inclined to cause problems for an audience. If someone speaks in a monotonous tone over a long period of time, people construe that they're not really interested in their material. When a speaker uses a high-pitched voice, an audience may not take that speaker very seriously. And when a person speaks rapidly, he or she may be defined as impatient or aggressive. So unless you want your soft voice to indicate that you are not confident or your breathy voice to represent you as sexy, study the next section on using a professional voice.

Using a Professional Voice

Thirty percent of the American public is unhappy with the way their voice sounds. The difference between you and the majority of people is that you can follow three simple steps to master a professional voice. Read on to find out how varying the volume, rate, and pitch of your voice can change the way you sound.

Volume

If you've ever been told or told someone else to speak up, join the club. Speaking loud enough so that an audience can hear you seems to be the most important factor in controlling your voice. By standing erect and relaxing, you should be able to project to an audience of less than 200 people. If you're addressing more than 200 people, use a microphone.

Concentrate on being loud enough so that everyone can hear you, and on varying the loudness of your voice. If you're discussing a private situation, you can speak softer for effect. When you are talking about an exciting invention, increase the volume of your voice. The point is to vary the loudness of your voice.

Rate

Public speakers deliver about 120 to 150 words per minute. Novice speakers have a tendency to speak very quickly, so just remember to go slow enough to be heard. You also need to speak a bit slower if you're addressing a large crowd as opposed to a few people.

You know you're speaking too fast if you're gasping for breath or running your words together. And if you find that people are becoming bored or constantly requesting that you get to the point, then you may want to speed up your delivery.

Besides varying the speed of your delivery, you should utilize pauses in your verbal delivery. If you've delivered a particularly important point or quotation, you can pause for four seconds to let the audience reflect on the significance of what you've said. Get in the habit of asking a rhetorical question or stating a startling statistic and then pausing. Pauses can be the punctuation marks of speech.

Pitch

The third aspect of your voice is your pitch, or the high and low tones of your voice. Ideally, you should vary the pitch to create inflection in your voice. Most audiences find a monotone or one-pitch voice particularly irritating; aim for a middle pitch for most of your talking and work to vary the tone of your voice.

If you've decided that you want to change a particularly squeaky, husky, or gentle voice, you can begin by using a tape recorder. Tape yourself using higher and lower voices. Find a voice that you like and then emulate the sound repeatedly until it becomes natural.

Also get into the habit of analyzing your voice for voice-downers. Voice-downers would include verbal delivery that seems rushed, irritated, phony, or apathetic. A positive voice in business projects energy and enthusiasm. If, after several

REMINDERS TO IMPROVE YOUR VOICE

1. Speak loudly enough so that everyone can hear you.
2. Vary the loudness, pitch, and rate of your voice depending upon your material.
3. Use pauses as punctuation marks for your voice.
4. Use a positive and enthusiastic voice.

attempts, you need additional help to change your voice, find a competent communication consultant or speech therapist for assistance.

EVERYONE MAKES MISTAKES

There will probably be numerous times that you will make a mistake when you're delivering a speech. When a mistake occurs, take it in stride. Effective communicators can handle difficult and embarrassing situations.

Let's say that you mentioned the wrong business in the introduction of your speech. Once you recognize your mistake, address your error. Don't try to pass over a mistake thinking no one will notice it. Someone always will. Apologize if it's necessary.

If you've underestimated a profit by $10,000 dollars, apologize for the inaccuracy. And, if it's at all possible, use humor. When you've made a mistake, recognize that it can't be undone, make things right, and then move on.

PRACTICE POSITIVE THOUGHTS

Many speech consultants say that mastery of positive thinking has a remarkable effect on the way a person delivers presentations as well as how he or she views life. The theory is that optimism breeds positive self-esteem which, in turn, results in a confident verbal and nonverbal delivery.

Positive thinking means eradicating counterproductive thoughts from your mind. Replace "I will never come across effectively" with "I will be effective." Being

---

WORDS FROM THE WISE

"The first thing to keep in mind is that we should speak through the throat and not from it. A musical quality of voice depends chiefly upon directing the tone toward the hard palate or the bony arch above the upper teeth. From this part of the mouth the voice acquires much of its resonance."

—*Grenville Kleiser*

"Ninety percent of all the friction of daily life is caused by mere tone of voice. When a man speaks, his words convey his thoughts and his tone conveys his mood."

—*Lord Chesterfield*

TRUE STORY

Margaret Hamilton was a vice president of a major bank. She was a financial wizard but according to her employees, she lacked people skills. Ms. Hamilton hired a communication consultant to analyze her interpersonal skills and figure out what to do.

The consultant videotaped Margaret in meetings, interviews, and giving speeches. Then both Margaret and the consultant analyzed the interactions. What Margaret saw on tape was not the way she pictured herself. "I always thought that I was assertive," said Margaret "but what I saw was a very aggressive person."

After two months of working on becoming assertive rather than aggressive, Margaret was a different person both on and off the videotape.

---

aware and then consciously controlling your thoughts will have an effect on your delivery.

VIDEOTAPING YOUR DELIVERY

One of the best ways to analyze your presentation skills is by videotaping yourself. In fact many CEOs, politicians, and other leaders routinely study their presentations on videotape. When you see yourself talking in a meeting, lecture, interview, or any other communication situation, it's much easier to analyze your skills objectively and thus pinpoint your strengths and weaknesses.

Now here's your opportunity to show off your skills. Complete the chapter by filling out the exercises and answers.

EXERCISES

A. Analyze a videotape of yourself. How is your nonverbal delivery (posture, clothing, gestures, facial expressions) and your verbal delivery (volume, rate, and pitch)? If there is something you want to change, set tangible goals for accomplishing the task. For example, if you decide to slow down your delivery and sound less rushed, set a time limit of approximately one month to reach that goal.

WORDS FROM THE WISE

"Thinking good thoughts, positive and cheerful thoughts, will improve the way you feel. What affects your mind also affects your body."

—*Clement Stone*

B. Select a role model on television, in film, or in person. What aspects of that person's delivery would you like to emulate? Are his or her gestures smooth and reinforcing? Is there something particularly attractive about the speaking voice? Analyze the person's delivery. Try to incorporate the positive aspects of that person's delivery into your own style.

Quiz

1. What are four aspects of body language?
2. What are three rules for clothing at work?
3. What should you do if you make a mistake when you're speaking?
4. What can you do to improve your nonverbal delivery?
5. What can you do to improve your verbal delivery?

Answer Key

1. Four aspects of body language include:
   a. Facial expressions
   b. Clothing
   c. Gestures
   d. Proximity or space between people
2. Rules about your clothing include:
   a. Appropriate
   b. Comfortable
   c. Clean
3. When you make a mistake:
   a. Admit you made a mistake.
   b. Correct the error.
   c. Use humor if appropriate.
4. To improve your nonverbal delivery, you can:
   a. Appear natural.

b. Coordinate your gestures and movement with what you say.

c. Don't overdo either gestures or movement.

5. To improve your verbal delivery:

a. Speak loud enough so that everyone can hear.

b. Vary your pitch, rate, and loudness.

c. Use pauses as punctuation points.

d. Use a positive and enthusiastic voice.

NEXT STEP

Congratulations on another great job! Now that you have completed this lesson, you're ready for the next chapter on *The Importance of Audiovisual Aids.* Good luck and keep up the good work!

CHAPTER 10

THE IMPORTANCE OF AUDIOVISUAL AIDS

No matter how interesting the topic of your speech is, at one time or another, your audience's attention may begin to wane. Perhaps your audience just doesn't grasp what you're saying about the increase in last year's profits. Or maybe they're just tired of looking at you and only you. Whatever the reason, it is your responsibility to keep your presentation interesting and clear so that your audience will attend to what you say.

One way to maintain interest is by incorporating audiovisual aids into your speech. Studies reveal that audiences comprehend and retain information better and longer if audiovisual aids are used. When audiovisual aids are used correctly, they can be an effective way to explain and reinforce valuable information. But, when used incorrectly, aids can turn a mediocre speech into a disaster.

One of the most positive aspects of using audiovisual aids is that anyone can learn to use them. It doesn't take a rocket scientist or a computer genius to create and use most audiovisual soft- and hardware. Just incorporate the following information into your presentation skills, and you too can become a pro at using audiovisual aids.

USING AUDIOVISUAL AIDS

The first thing you need to consider is whether you really need to use an audiovisual aid. An aid is an excellent way to enhance or complement a point that you've made in your speech, but it should never be used as a substitute for a well-prepared speech. An audiovisual aid will never compensate for inadequate evidence or poor organization. What aids will provide is the icing on the cake or that extra-special touch that will transform a good presentation into a great one.

So rather than automatically deciding to incorporate an audiovisual aid into a presentation, think about whether it will help you to explain a complex thought or reinforce the central idea of your speech. You may conclude that it's best to forgo the aid and speak throughout your five-minute presentation.

Second, consider the type of audiovisual aid you want to use. The most frequently used audiovisual aids include the flip chart, overhead projector, handout, and videotape. While there are advantages and disadvantages for using each type, you need to contemplate which aid is best suited for your material. If you're presenting information on the company's budget to 100 people, you should consider using an overhead projector. You could create two transparencies: one with the total budget and the second as a pie chart with allocations for various departments' budgets.

The point is that you must decide which audiovisual aid is most appropriate for your material. You would select videotape as your medium to capture the three-dimensional beauty and excitement of a parachute jumping experience, not because most people watch a lot of television. Just ask yourself what type of aid would present your material in the most clear and interesting manner.

Third, consider your budget. As a rule, making a flip chart is inexpensive, and production of a videotape is exorbitant. Figure out exactly how much money you can spend on your aid. If you hire out for audiovisual aid production, be specific about the length of your tape and the number of copies. Quotes may vary considerably according to a few minutes or inches.

Fourth, keep your audiovisual aids simple. If you remember that you, not the audiovisual aid, are the star, you may be able to keep things in the proper perspective. Accolades should occur as a result of your speech, not because of your award-winning videotapes or graphics. Each aid should contain one concept, and never

REMINDERS FOR USING AUDIOVISUAL AIDS

1. Ask yourself whether you really need to use the audiovisual aid. An audiovisual aid should enhance your speech, not replace it.
2. Select the type of audiovisual aid that's best suited for your material.
3. Make sure that your budget can support the cost of your audiovisual aid.
4. Keep your audiovisual aid simple. One concept per aid is the limit.
5. Don't stand between your audience and the aid.
6. Keep the aid hidden. Show it and then put it away.
7. Explain everything. Label your aids and make sure your audience understands what you show them.

include more than two types of audiovisual aids in one speech. Covering more than one concept and using more than two audiovisual aids is overkill for most audiences.

Fifth, never stand between your aid and the audience. Have you ever attended a speech where the speaker blocked you from seeing the information on a visual aid? Learn from someone else's mistakes and don't create such a frustrating experience for your audience.

Sixth, keep your aid hidden or covered until you use it. Show it as you discuss its significance and then put it away. If you leave the aid visible throughout your whole speech, your audience may be more concerned about it than about listening to you.

Finally, never assume that your audience understands anything about your audiovisual aid. Title each aid and remember that you're the one who has spent hours with this aid, not them.

By observing these simple guidelines, you can improve the comprehension and retention of your presentation. Now let's take a closer look at specific audiovisual aids by beginning with the flip chart.

Flip Charts

Flip charts are the true workhorses of meetings and workshops. Mounted on an easel or other stand, flip charts are portable, cheap, simple to use, audience friendly, and nondisruptive of the speaker's delivery to an audience. Most of us can probably recall at least one occasion when a flip chart was beneficial in our comprehension of some information.

Perhaps you remember the meeting where your boss wanted feedback on the new billing system, so he wrote down your input on a chart. Then your department went through the list and prioritized each item. Or maybe you recall the flip chart with the bar graph depicting your company's profits over the last five years. You may recall how, after the speech, it was much easier to picture the bar graph than remember the actual statistics. The bottom line is that flip charts are a great tool in speechmaking.

Flip charts are perfect for a group of less than 50 people when you want immediate feedback. You only need to turn away from the audience for a few moments to write on a flip chart, and you can use the chart with the lights on. When you are speaking to a crowd of more than 50, use the larger image from an overhead projector so that everyone can see.

In order to make sure that each member of your audience can see the wording, letters must be at least one inch tall for every 15 feet a person is from the aid. It's also a good idea never to exceed 25 words on one sheet and to print your information as neatly as you can.

While the paper for flip charts is light and easy to manage, its weight and texture is not conducive to storing. Thus, if you have valuable information on your flip chart, make sure that you copy it onto another sheet. Finally, as is the case with all visual aids, remember to look at your audience, not your flip chart.

Overhead Projector

If your audience is more than 50 people but less than 300, an overhead projector may be your best choice for showing a visual aid. You can project your transparencies onto a screen, leave the lights on, and be able to continue eye contact with

REMINDERS FOR FLIP CHARTS

1. Use flip charts when you need to write down comments from your audience.
2. Use flip charts with no more than 50 people.
3. Print letters one inch high for every 15 feet of distance from the audience.
4. Bring two or more black pens to write with.
5. Look at your audience, not the chart.

REMINDERS FOR USING TRANSPARENCIES

1. Use only one concept per transparency. People will only be able to comprehend and retain one idea. More than 10 words on a transparency is overload.
2. Don't block the projector's light. People want to see the transparency, not your shadow. Use a pointer if you need to step to the side of the screen.
3. Look at your audience, not the screen. Be so familiar with your overhead transparency that you don't need to look at it.
4. Keep extra bulbs available just in case a bulb burns out. And, of course, know how to replace the bulb.
5. Use frames or slipcovers for your transparencies so they won't curl at the corners.
6. Know where you'll plug in your equipment. Make sure that you have an extension cord just in case the outlet is some distance away.

your audience. You do, however, need a room that can be darkened a bit in order for your transparency to be seen well.

Keep your overhead transparency out of sight until you use it; show it, and then put it away. Prevent the "snowstorm" from blinding your viewers by covering or turning off the projector when you aren't showing an image.

You can write on a clear transparency or use a premade visual. Overhead transparencies can be made from photographs, slides, or almost any written copy or design that you have. Line and bar graphs, cartoons, and drawings work particularly well as overhead transparencies. There are copy machines, software packages, and printing shops that can turn an idea or an image into an overhead transparency. Many new computer programs enable you to print a professional-looking transparency in no time at all.

Using an overhead transparency can be a perfect way to appear professional. Just remember to incorporate the reminders above into the creation and use of your overhead transparencies.

Videotape

One of the more exciting yet challenging visual aids is the videotape. Videotape enables an audience to transcend their reality by entering a three-dimensional fantasy. An average American will be impressed with your ability to incorporate a

REMINDERS FOR VIDEOTAPE

1. Know how to use the videotape player. Make sure the videotape is cued up and was originally taped at the appropriate speed.
2. Be familiar with the electrical sockets and light controls. You may end up being the person who controls the lights.
3. Turn the set on when you're going to use the tape. Make sure the volume is down. Turn off the set when you're done with it. Don't leave the set on.
4. Never try to talk over the narration on a videotape. The same rule applies to trying to talk over a song with lyrics.
5. Rehearse your speech at least once with the videotape.

favorite recreational pastime into a business speech. With television being a seven-hour-a-day presence in the average American home, audiences generally enjoy the combination of work and video.

Until you've had a lot of practice incorporating a videotape into the middle of your speech, it's best to use a tape at the beginning or end of your speech. Just imagine, before your sales speech for a Caribbean cruise ship, you show a three-minute edited videotape of the gorgeous beauty of the scenery. With a breathtaking introduction to what you want to sell, your audience is destined to listen to you.

Or at the end of your speech honoring your supervisor's retirement, you could leave your audience with a videotaped montage of 20 years of photographs taken at work. If nothing else, they'll remember the tape. Just remember the list of videotape reminders.

Handouts

For most businesspeople, handouts are the most frequently used visual aids. A handout can take the form of a report, plan, projection, or reminder. There are certain situations in business when you must have a handout for your audience, no matter how small or large.

Any time that you chair a meeting, make sure that you have a handout of an agenda for the group. If possible, try to distribute the agenda prior to the meeting so that people will have a chance to preview important items. If you will be referring to a detailed budget, legal document, or any other complex document, always make a handout.

You will need a handout for any presentation that involves technical, financial, or complicated information that your audience needs. If you're explaining the five steps in operating a color copy machine, you should have a diagram of the machine with directions available for the audience. Likewise, the latest copy of a detailed budget calls for a handout. And if you're going over the five basic parts of a business letter to your colleagues, it would probably be in everyone's best interests to have a sample business letter available.

A written semiannual or annual report should be available at the time of an oral presentation. The disadvantage of handing the report out before the speech is that everyone may be looking at the written form and not paying attention to the speaker. This seems to apply to any distribution of a visual aid while a speech is being delivered. Once you hand out the photographs, model, or brochure, the attention of the audience turns to that aid. So think twice about the timing before you pass around your audiovisual aid.

CONTENT OF VISUAL AIDS

Once you've decided the type of visual aid you're going to use and the subject of that aid, you'll need to determine exactly what the content will look like. No matter what the content of your visual aid will be, there are a few general guidelines that you need to follow.

If you decide to use color in your audiovisual aid (and you *should* use color for variety), limit the number of colors to three. While you can use various *saturations* of those three colors if you're making a bar graph on a transparency, for example, never exceed that maximum number. Because research indicates that black is the most noticeable color, print your title in black.

If you are planning to use more than two visual aids, coordinate the colors. For example, when you're showing 20 transparencies, you could use black, violet, and blue on all the visuals. Your presentation will appear more organized if your audiovisual aids appear as a package.

If you're using a lot of aids, try to make them as creative and original as possible. Put yourself in the shoes of your audience and imagine looking at the same black-and-white screen with words. There's a happy medium between boring audiovisual aids and artistic masterpieces. Find the middle ground and create transparencies that are engaging and yet supplement your spoken material.

If your business has a logo, it's a good idea to include it somewhere on your audiovisual aids. Your could place it on the first or last overhead transparency, at the end of the videotape, or on the first page of your handout. Your logo is just another way to remind your audience who is responsible for your presentation.

Graphics

When you transfer an idea to a pictorial representation that can be used as an audiovisual aid, you have created a graphic. Graphics include illustrations, charts, and graphs. Consider each type of graphic carefully before you spend time or money on the preparation of your visual aid.

Illustrations can be drawings, photographs, or diagrams. Illustrations can be created manually, generated by computer, or copied from an original source onto a transparency, slide, or poster board. No matter which way your illustration is made, the bottom line is to use simplicity and creativity in its design.

Sales Dept - Allocation of Total Budget

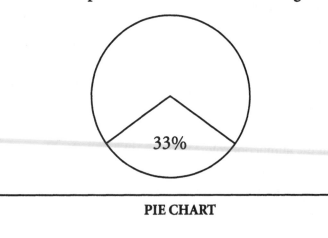

33%

PIE CHART

Bright Bank Organization

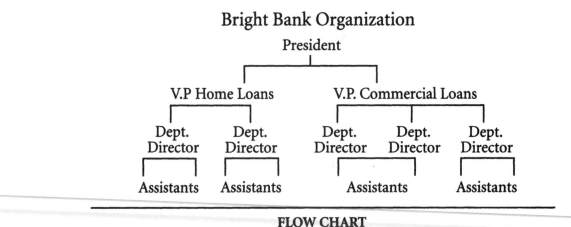

FLOW CHART

Charts can express numerical and organizational information. Pie charts are frequently used to show the distribution of a budget, flow charts demonstrate the organizational structure within a company, and time charts list projects and their completion dates.

Graphs are used to show the relationship between some numerical information. Bar graphs use parallel lines or rectangular boxes to demonstrate some quantifiable data; line graphs are generally used to show increase or decrease over time. Give each graph a title, limit the number of bars and lines to five, and keep them simple.

Jude McMann Account

February Marketing Goals

Activities for Jean and Jess	Objectives Approved	Logo DRAFT Ready	Brochure DRAFT Ready	Final Logo & Brochure Prepared	Press Release & Info Sheet Ready	Customer Mailing Completed
	2/5	2/8	2/9	2/15	2/17	2/28

TIME CHART

Greene's Clients

BAR GRAPH

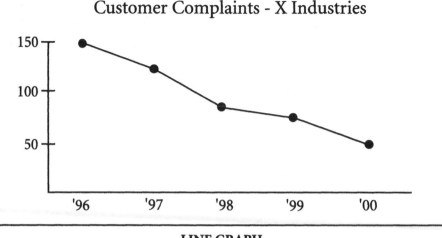

LINE GRAPH

Start examining the graphics that surround you. Incorporate the most effective ideas into your next graphics.

Evaluating Your Audiovisual Aids

Consider these three questions when evaluating the effectiveness of a visual aid:

First, ask yourself, is the audiovisual aid necessary? Be sure that your aid supplements or explains your speech. Never include an audiovisual aid because of a lack of material or fear of speaking.

Second, can you understand the aid? If you can't read the words or decipher the diagram, then it's highly unlikely that your audience will be able to. Check to make sure that you can see the aid from any location in your room.

Third, does the audiovisual aid look professional? People make first impressions quickly. Don't let your audience negatively judge your speech because of an amateurish-looking aid.

The bottom line is that an effective aid will make a good speech great, while a poor aid will make a good speech worse. Spend time on your aids and plan a great presentation each time you speak.

WORDS FROM THE WISE

"One picture is worth a thousand words."

—*Chinese proverb*

REMINDERS FOR EVALUATING AIDS

1. Is it necessary?
2. Can you understand it?
3. Does it look professional?

Once again you're almost done with another chapter. Before you move on to the next step, you'll need to complete the exercises and questions. And as always, apply what you've read in your life and career.

EXERCISES

A. Incorporate one audiovisual aid into your next presentation. After the talk, analyze what you did correctly and what you could have done better.
B. Analyze a weatherperson's use of audiovisual aids. Who does the weather-caster keep eye contact with? What does the person use as a pointer? How could the weathercast be better?

Quiz

1. What are four types of audiovisual aids?
2. What should you remember when using a visual aid?
3. What are three types of graphics?
4. What questions could you ask to analyze the effectiveness of your audiovisual aids?

Answer Key

1. The four types of audiovisual aids include:
   a. Flip charts
   b. Overhead transparency
   c. Videotapes
   d. Handouts
2. Four things to remember when using an audiovisual aid include:
   a. Don't stand in front of the audiovisual aid.
   b. Keep them simple.

      c.   Show them and then put them away.

      d.   Make sure that you need the visual aid.

3. Graphics include illustrations, charts, and graphs.

NEXT STEP

Once again, a great job! Keep up the good work on the next chapter, *It's Important To Listen.*

CHAPTER | 11

IT'S IMPORTANT
TO LISTEN

How many times in business have you heard
the following statements or questions?

- What did you say your address was?
- Oh, we don't have your check ready. Miscommunication on our
  part.
- Sorry. Our receptionist was given the wrong information.
- My fault. I was thinking about something else.
- Now what was that problem again?

If you've ever been part of a conversation that included the previous
remarks, then count yourself among thousands of customers who each
day are given incomplete or incorrect information. What's particularly
alarming is that many of the problems could be prevented if someone
just would LISTEN. It's true!

Many problems occur in business because employees aren't attending to the task of listening. What's more, this trend is disturbing because research indicates that some of the most successful salespeople and executives are those who listen most effectively. According to Thomas J. Peters, author of *In Search of Excellence*, "Attention to employees has the dominant impact on productivity." Most people love to be listened to. Over the past 10 years in the United States, more money has been spent on talking to psychologists, psychiatrists, and counselors than in any other decade. What this means is that in our society, listening is a valuable skill.

It's an interesting fact that most people think of listening as a passive activity and talking as an active one. And in the world of business, most people would agree that "active" is where it's at. Listening, however, is an extremely active activity. Think of the patience that was involved when you listened to an irate customer complain about a product. Or remember when a customer took forever to describe exactly what she was looking for? Listening takes patience, skill, and energy.

The positive thing about listening is that when you master the skills involved in truly hearing what someone says, it pays off for you and your business. The result: you remember your boss's instructions from your last meeting, you recall the directions for that special order, or you know who to contact with a great idea. As Voltaire, a famous French philosopher, once said, "When I listen I have the power. When I speak, I give it away." If you get in the habit of listening in a professional manner, you can eliminate miscommunication problems, increasing your value at work.

WHY DON'T WE LISTEN

There are many times that we perceive sounds but we aren't converting the spoken word into meaning in our minds. In other words, there are situations when we just don't listen. Many people don't listen because they're too busy with their intrapersonal communication (what they're telling themselves). Because their thoughts are concerned with being mad, bored, or stressed, they don't listen to what someone is saying; some authors refer to this phenomenon as *internal noise*. Internal noise occurs when you are so preoccupied with how you feel that you aren't aware of what someone is trying to communicate.

Sometimes when people are too concerned about how they've come across to someone else, they expend more energy trying to *look* like they're listening than if they were actually listening. Ironic, isn't it? But we've all been in an interview,

WORDS FROM THE WISE

"Formula for handling people:
1. Listen to the other person's story.
2. Listen to the other person's full story.
3. Listen to the other person's full story first."

—General George Marshall

"I like to listen, I have learned a great deal from listening carefully. Most people never listen."

—Ernest Hemingway

meeting, or social hour before a convention, when we are so concerned about how we look or what we'll say that we just don't listen.

Another reason that people don't listen is because there is too much external noise around them. Maybe there is too much traffic outside or people are yelling in the hall. Perhaps the lights are too bright or the chairs too hard. Or it could be that the speaker's nonverbal habit of playing with his paper clip is interfering with your listening. There are both visual and auditory types of external "noise" that hinder listening.

A third reason that people don't listen is because they're preoccupied with their own view on what is being said. When a new idea or an opposing view is expressed, these individuals may think, "I've heard that before," "There's no point in listening to this," or "I'm sure I know everything that's going to be said." They become close-minded and are thus shut off from any different or new ideas. The best approach to listening is to keep an open mind. You just never know when listening with an open mind may lead to a creative idea or a novel approach to doing business.

The final reason that people don't listen is because most people's minds can process approximately 500 words per minute, whereas while most people speak, on average, 120 to 150 words per minute. This difference means that because most people's minds work faster than speakers can talk, listeners' minds may wander.

Whatever the reasons, there are times when most people don't listen. That's fine when it's your leisure time, but when you're being paid to work, listening is an important skill that you need to master. Analyze your listening skills by reviewing the following reasons why people don't listen:

REASONS FOR INEFFECTIVE LISTENING

1. Listening is blocked by internal noise or intrapersonal communication.
2. Listening is blocked by external noise.
3. Preconceived ideas and judgments hinder listening.
4. Most people think faster than someone can talk.

HOW TO LISTEN EFFECTIVELY

We all are guilty of not listening to a customer or our boss at some time during our life at work. So we all can improve our listening skills by following some simple yet effective guidelines.

One of the most important things that you can do to improve the quality of your listening is to have a specific objective or purpose for listening. When you are listening to a customer's complaint, know that your objective is to solve a problem and empathize with that person. During your annual evaluation session with your supervisor, listen for your strengths, weaknesses, and what your boss wants you to do. And when you are receiving computer instruction, listen so that you will be able to perform a specific computer task.

Second, listen with an open mind. When you go into a situation thinking that you will not learn anything or that you have all the answers, you are shutting yourself off from effective listening and learning.

Third, avoid jumping to conclusions about the speaker and what's being said. Listen to the total message before you draw your conclusions. Give a speaker a chance to develop an argument and substantiate major points. While there is a tendency to make snap judgments on the basis of an initial impression, it's in the best interest of you and your business not to label or stereotype someone after a few minutes.

Fourth, when you listen to someone, face the speaker and develop eye contact. Eliminate any external barriers to listening such as a distracting radio, a blinding light, or a humming computer terminal. Don't be guilty of customers' common complaint that an employee didn't look at them.

Fifth, don't interrupt people when they're trying to talk. There are no two ways about it—interrupting is rude. You may think that you're more skillful or more qualified to answer for another person, but guess what? You're not. Let the other person talk.

REMINDERS FOR LISTENING

1. Always have a purpose for listening.
2. Eliminate both external and internal noise.
3. Keep an open mind and avoid preconceived judgments.
4. Provide feedback to the speaker.
5. Never interrupt.
6. Write down notes in order to jog your memory later.

Sixth, get into the habit of providing feedback to the speaker. When you nod your head up and down or provide verbal responses, you are reminding your speaker and yourself that you are attending to the message. It's best to use neutral statements such as, "I understand what you're saying" and "So that's how you feel about it" until the speaker has completed his or her complete explanation. Or you can paraphrase something that has been said to make sure that you fully understand the idea. Withhold your judgments, however, until the other person has completed talking.

Seventh, be prepared to listen. If you're going to listen to a speech on this year's marketing successes, make sure that you are familiar with both this and last year's marketing objectives and strategies. Or if you are attending a panel discussion on the annual report, make sure that you have read the whole written document.

Eighth, keep a small notebook or laptop with you at all times to record important times, dates, and other business information. Because you cannot be expected to remember everything, a written document will be helpful to jog your memory.

Now that you've finished reading this information, complete the following exercises and quiz.

EXERCISES

A. Make a plan for improving your listening. Write down two situations where you should improve your listening skills. Make sure you also record *why* you need to improve your skills. Then make a concerted effort to improve your listening.

B. Take notes at your next meeting. If you don't understand something, ask questions or paraphrase what was said. Later analyze the clarity and effectiveness of what was said.

Quiz

1. Why don't people listen?
2. How can you become a more effective listener?

Answers

1. People don't listen because they are:
   a. Distracted by external or internal noise
   b. Concerned about what they'll say next
   c. Prejudiced, narrow-minded, or opinionated
   d. Bored, stressed, tired
2. You can become a better listener if you:
   a. Have a purpose for listening
   b. Face people and use eye contact
   c. Get rid of external barriers
   d. Stop interrupting
   e. Provide feedback

NEXT STEP

Well, you've done it again! You've completed this chapter and now you're ready to move on to Chapter 12, *Evaluating Your Performance*. Remember that with listening, as well as with the other presentation skills in this book, practice makes perfect.

CHAPTER | 12

EVALUATING YOUR PERFORMANCE

There are three effective ways to test the strength of your message. First, carry out a self-critique. Whenever possible, write down a detailed self-analysis, but if you don't have a lot of time, just concentrate on the basic strengths and weaknesses of your presentation. Also include what you can do better for the next presentation you give.

The second way to analyze your presentations is to record them on videotape. After viewing the tape, you'll be able to determine your strengths, weaknesses, and areas to focus on for improvement. And you'll also have permanent documentation of your performance that can be used to compare with later presentations.

The third means of analysis is to get feedback from your audience. This could be done by informally asking people how you're coming across, or you could administer a formal survey asking participants to address specific criteria regarding your presentation. When you ask your audience to evaluate your presentation, you're gaining objectivity and ultimately finding out if you reached them with your message. It won't take you long to realize that you're probably your own worst critic and that others have a more tolerant opinion of your skills than you.

The following section deals with specific, formal criteria that you, a colleague, or a friend could use when critiquing your presentations. These criteria can also be used to evaluate others. You'll find that when you evaluate other speeches, you will be able to learn from others' mistakes and accomplishments.

EVALUATION CRITERIA

The four basic categories for evaluation of a presentation include: content, delivery, audiovisual aids, and preparation. If these categories sound familiar, great! We've discussed these areas in previous chapters, so you should be familiar with some of this material.

Content

The words you use, the main points you make, and the evidence you include—these factors make up the content, or text, of your presentation. More specifically, when we evaluate the content of a presentation, we examine the introduction, body, and conclusion. The following sections discuss the approaches to take in evaluating each part of a presentation.

Evaluating the Introduction

There are two important questions to ask when evaluating an introduction. First, look at whether the speaker engaged the audience with an interesting quotation,

WORDS FROM THE WISE

" 'Let a man examine himself.' That sentence asks a man to turn inward some of the attention he pours on the outside. 'Be honest with yourself,' it says. 'Examine your motives, your concerns, your fears, in your own quietude. You can be completely honest. You have only yourself in this consultation. You don't have to rationalize or try to hide anything. No one is listening but you. You don't have to strain to get someone else to understand.' When sincerity and candor are present, such a self-examination can be healthful, curative."

—*L.D. Ditzen*

example, fact, or statistic. There's a big difference between grabbing the audience's attention in the beginning of the presentation and, on the other hand, introducing the topic.

The second area in analyzing the introduction is to determine whether the purpose of the presentation was adequately covered. The introduction should let the audience know exactly where the speech is headed. There should be no doubt about the specific purpose. By stating the specific purpose you are giving the audience a reason to listen. And as we know from Chapter 11, a reason to listen will increase your audience's listening abilities. An effective introduction starts things off with a bang and provides an overview of where you're headed.

Ask yourself the following questions about an introduction:

1. Did the introduction engage your attention?
2. Did the introduction include a specific purpose?

Evaluating the Body

The first thing you should note about the body or main section is whether the main points are clear. Are you able to recognize the five steps in the new data entry program? Can you state the problem and solution in staffing interns? If you're having difficulty recalling the major points of the presentation, then there probably is a clarity problem.

Next, it's important to have a well-organized body. If your specific purpose is to persuade your audience that the Sales Department needs new computers, you probably want to use a problem–solution structure. By establishing that the current computers were not functioning 50% of the workday and that customers had a wait time of up to five minutes, you've identified a problem. Moving on to the solution phase, you could determine that the only solution would be to purchase computers for the department. A relatively simple yet effective structure works best in this situation.

As another example, if you're giving a speech on the history of your business, you probably want to use a chronological pattern and stay on a timeline from beginning to the present. Audiences are able to grasp the historical aspect more easily that way.

Third, you want to make sure that the major points are well supported. The speaker can use evidence to prove his or her points. If a speaker states that there should be no sales tax, the audience deserves to know why not. Evidence demonstrates that there should, in fact, be no tax. By using evidence, you avoid the "I think" speech that only you can understand and appreciate.

Fourth, you need to evaluate the language. If there are sexist or racist remarks, somebody needs to tell the speaker that the law mandates that there be no discrimination in business. If a speaker uses alienating terminology, words, or examples, that speaker isn't thinking about the audience's perspective.

In addition, if a speaker uses substandard English or incorrect grammar, you may have trouble recognizing them as credible sources. The language a speaker uses can make a world of difference regarding an audience's perception of that speech.

Finally, audience members need to ask whether they have learned what they were told they would learn. Did the body of information satisfy the specific purpose of the introduction? Was the audience persuaded or informed about a topic? Did the main points accomplish the objective of the speech? An effective speech will definitely contain a body that achieves these goals.

In review, when evaluating the body of a speech, look at the following criteria:

1. Are the main points clear?
2. Were the major points well organized?
3. Was the language appropriate?
4. Were the main points well supported?
5. Did the speech accomplish its purpose?

Evaluating the Conclusion

There are two important points to remember in your conclusion. The first is that you need to remind your audience of the specific purpose of your presentation. When you say, "Now that I have explained the five myths of the import-export business...," you're reminding your audience that you've spent the last hour discussing something with them (your specific purpose).

You also need to leave the audience with something memorable. After 10 minutes discussing the benefits of loving your job, you conclude with the following:

Over the last 10 minutes, I have discussed the benefits of really liking your job. We talked about the effect a positive image of work has on your productivity, creativity, and stress levels. As we've seen today, the overall benefits of a positive attitude toward work are monumental. Let me sum up this speech by reading a quotation by F.H. Ecker, former chairperson of Metropolitan Life: "I don't think anybody has invented a pastime that's as much fun, or keeps you as young, as a good job." Thank you for inviting me to speak to you today.

Make sure that a speech leaves you with a worthwhile and memorable quotation, example, or challenge. Ask yourself the following questions about a conclusion:

1. Does the conclusion summarize the objective of the speech?
2. Does the conclusion leave you with some special message?

Delivery

A speaker's delivery can be examined by looking at both the nonverbal and verbal presentation. Once again, if this information sounds familiar, good, because we'll be reviewing some delivery points we covered in a previous chapter.

A speaker's nonverbal delivery involves the way someone presents him- or herself without talking. The main nonverbal areas include facial expression, gestures, posture, and clothing. Think about these items when critiquing nonverbal delivery:

1. Does a speaker develop and maintain appropriate eye contact with the audience?
2. Are gestures used to reinforce a point?
3. Was movement used appropriately?
4. Is the speaker's appearance appropriate and comfortable?
5. Is the speaker's posture relaxed yet professional?
6. Was there anything distracting about the nonverbal delivery?

The verbal delivery is comprised of the volume, pitch, rate, and use of pauses and nonfluencies. You could ask the following questions about the verbal delivery:

1. Is the speaker loud enough so that everyone in the room can hear?
2. Does the speaker address the audience in a clear and coherent manner?
3. Is there any distracting aspect to the speaker's voice?
4. Is the speaker using a normal rate of delivery? Too fast? Too slow?
5. Are nonfluencies (use of *um, ah, er,* etc.) interfering with the speech?
6. Are pauses being used effectively?

Audiovisual Aids

The following list of questions will help you to evaluate the effectiveness of audio-visual aids:

1. Is the audiovisual aid necessary?
2. Does the audiovisual aid enhance or supplement an important point?
3. Are the audiovisual aids neat and easy to read?
4. Is the spelling and grammar correct?
5. Are the equipment and visuals well operated?
6. Did I learn something from the audiovisual aid?

Audiovisual aids can certainly enhance a speech. The important thing is to keep them simple and effective.

Preparation

Preparation has to do with the amount of planning that you put into your speech prior to its delivery. An audience will always know—and resent it—when little preparation has gone into a presentation. Ask yourself the following questions about preparation:

1. Was the speech well thought out?
2. Did the speaker begin and end on time?
3. Was there a good distribution of time for each topic?
4. Does the speaker know the material?
5. Was the speaker well rehearsed?
6. Was the speaker relaxed and confident?
7. Did the speaker relate to the audience?
8. Was the speaker enthusiastic or inspiring?

Success in speechmaking involves developing a rapport with an audience. So get into the habit of being prepared and connecting with your audience.

SELF-CRITIQUE

Every speech that you deliver should be followed by a self-critique. Many people keep a journal about their progress, and other speakers have their videotapes to turn to. At the very least, complete a self-critique 50% of the time over the period of a year. You should include the following questions in your self-critique:

1. Overall, how did I feel about the speech?
2. What were my strengths?
3. What were my weaknesses?
4. What should have spent more time on?
5. Next time I will work to improve...

Improvement comes when you identify a flaw in your presentation, work to change it, and continue to incorporate the new act into your day-to-day behavior. So keep analyzing and continue to become an even more effective speaker. The following form will assist you in evaluating both yourself and other speakers.

Evaluation can be an excellent means of improving your speeches. Take critiquing seriously and watch your skills soar. You should do well on the exercises and questions below.

EXERCISES

A. Videotape one of your speeches. Analyze your presentation according to the Speaker Critique Form in this chapter. Be sure to concentrate on the areas that you think are particularly strong or weak.
B. Evaluate another speaker according to the Speaker Critique Form. Begin your evaluation with a few criteria, and add more each time you evaluate someone.

Quiz

1. Explain at least ten criteria that you can use to evaluate a speech.
2. What's the advantage of completing a self-critique?

Answer Key

1. You can evaluate presentations according to the following criteria:
   a. Was the introduction engaging?
   b. Were the main points clear?
   c. Was an effective organization used?

SPEAKER CRITIQUE FORM

Speaker's name_____

Date_____   Topic_____

Please write comments for each of the following areas:

Content
Was there an interesting introduction?
Did the introduction contain a specific purpose?
Were the main points clear?
Were the major points well organized?
Was the language appropriate?
Were the main points well supported?
Did the speech accomplish its purpose?
Did the conclusion summarize the objective of the speech?
Did the conclusion leave you with something worthwhile?

Delivery
Did the speaker develop and maintain appropriate eye contact?
Were gestures used to reinforce a point?
Was the speaker's appearance appropriate and comfortable?
Was the speaker's posture relaxed yet professional?
Was there anything distracting about the delivery?
Was the speaker loud enough?
Was the speaker using a normal rate of delivery?
Were nonfluencies interfering with the speech?
Were pauses being used effectively?

Audiovisual Aids
Was the audiovisual aid necessary?
Did the audiovisual aid enhance or supplement an important point?
Were the visuals easy to read?
Were the spelling and grammar correct?
Were the equipment and audiovisuals well operated?
Did I learn anything from the audiovisual aid?

Preparation
Was the speech well thought out?
Did the speaker begin and end on time?
Was there a fair distribution of time spent on main points?
Did the speaker know the material?
Was the speaker well rehearsed?
Was the speaker relaxed and confident?
Did the speaker relate well to the audience?
Was the speaker enthusiastic or inspiring?

    d. Were the major points supported with evidence?

    e. Did the conclusion restate the specific purpose of the speech?

    f. Did the conclusion leave you with something worthwhile?

    g. Were the visual aids easy to read?

    h. Were the audiovisual aids necessary?

    i. Did you learn something from the audiovisual aids?

    j. Did the speaker seem prepared and rehearsed?

2. A self-critique gives you the opportunity to evaluate yourself and determine what skills you need to maintain and which ones may need work. You can examine your speeches over a period of time and be pleased with your great improvement!

NEXT STEP

Good work on this chapter! You're ready to move on to Chapter 13, *Increasing Your Vocabulary.*

CHAPTER | 13

INCREASING YOUR VOCABULARY

Your vocabulary says a lot about you and your business. Your words are a reflection of who you are and what's going on in your mind. Words indicate whether someone is thinking clearly or his or her mind processes are a little foggy. Your vocabulary tells other people whether you are bright, eager to please, or misinformed.

A great vocabulary is not composed of thousands of words that no one understands. Words such as *stentorian* and *mendicant* will probably have no meaning to most people. An effective vocabulary is based, however, on words that enable you to convey your thoughts in a clear manner. Effective vocabularies are ones that use relatively simple words to state an idea, direction, or question.

It's a fallacy that our vocabularies are completely formed by the time we are adults. If a person has been taught to value words since childhood, increasing his or her vocabulary as an adult will probably be a relatively easy task. But it has also been proven that adults can learn and use new

WORDS FROM THE WISE

"A large stock of words will be of practical value to you in your daily occupation and enhance your power of expression in speech and writing."

—*Grenville Kleiser*

words well into their 80s. Research also demonstrates that the ability to increase one's vocabulary is strongly correlated to a person's desire to learn new words.

So, whether you've carried on a love affair with words since you were a youngster or you've decided today that increasing your vocabulary will improve your job performance, this chapter is for you.

We'll begin the chapter with a discussion of guidelines that create an active environment for learning and remembering new words. Then we'll cover some root words that you can use when deciphering new words. And finally, we'll look at some similar words that create problems for most businesspeople. Let's begin with some guidelines for improving your vocabulary.

INCREASING YOUR WORD POWER

One of the simplest and most effective ways of increasing your vocabulary is to get in the habit of using a dictionary and thesaurus whenever you are working or reading. As you know, a dictionary contains an alphabetical list of words with their meanings, pronunciations, and etymologies or basic parts. Purchase a college dictionary (Random House Webster's is a good choice) and use it whenever you are unclear about the meaning of a word.

A thesaurus is a book that lists words and their synonyms. A *synonym* is a word that has the same definition as another word. When preparing your speech or business brief, you may find that you're using one particular word over and over. By looking in your thesaurus, you may find another word that will work in place of your original choice. For example, if you find that you're using the word *verbal* over and over again, a thesaurus might provide alternatives like *oral* or *spoken*.

A thesaurus also gives you a list of antonyms. *Antonyms* are words that mean the opposite of your original choice. Both dictionaries and thesauri are available in book form and on CD-ROM.

Second, read whenever you get a chance. Turn off the television and read a newspaper, magazine, or book. You'll find that the *New York Times, Wall Street Journal, U.S. News & World Report*, and *Time* will help to expand your vocabulary.

CHECKLIST FOR LEARNING NEW WORDS

✔ Plan to learn one word per week.

✔ Find a new word in a periodical or business report.

✔ Try to figure out the meaning from the context.

✔ Look the word up in a dictionary.

✔ Record the word in a vocabulary journal.

✔ Use the word in a verbal and written sentence.

✔ Use the word at least three times over the next week.

When you can understand and use every word in the *Times*, you may not need to work on your vocabulary any more!

Third, learn at least one word every week. Find a word in a periodical that you don't know and then strive to incorporate it into your repertoire. At first, try to figure out from the context in the sentence what a word means. Then look the word up in a dictionary. The next step is to use the new word in both a written and oral statement. Keep a journal or notebook full of your new words. Finally, use the word at least three times over the next week. Introducing a new word into your vocabulary is like developing a new muscle. You use it or you lose it.

Fourth, create mental pictures in your mind when you're having difficulty with a particular word. For example, if you are having problems learning the word *terse*, perhaps you could use the following steps to help you.

CHECKLIST FOR MAKING MENTAL PICTURES OF WORDS

✔ Review the definition of the word. Using the preceding example, *terse* means brief or short.

✔ Use your imagination. Perhaps you might associate *terse* with a street by your house called Terse Drive. You've always considered Terse Drive as a short street, a brief walk away from your house, so picture the drive in your mind when you read or hear the word *terse*.

✔ Make a flashcard with *terse* on one side and the definition and Terse Drive written the other side. Review your flashcards periodically and see if your mental picture helped you to remember the word.

REMINDERS FOR INCREASING YOUR VOCABULARY

1. Get in the habit of using a dictionary and thesaurus every day.
2. Read as much as you can. Look for new words.
3. Learn one word every week.
4. Create mental pictures of words that cause you difficulty.
5. Recognize that it takes time to increase your vocabulary. Be patient and persevere.

Fifth, recognize that there are very few achievements in life that are obtainable without work. Decide that you will increase your vocabulary, one word at a time, and follow through on your objective.

ROOT WORDS

Because there are thousands of words in English, it would be virtually impossible to learn all of them by looking them up in the dictionary. In addition to examining the context of a word to figure out its meaning, you can also get some help by looking at the root of the word.

The *root* is a part of the word that can be found in many words with similar meaning. If you know the meaning of the root, you can figure out the meaning of other, similar words. For example, the root *scribe* means to write and the words *scribble, postscript, manuscript,* and *scripture* are derived from that root. Examine the list of roots, their meanings, and words that are based on those roots on the next page.

By looking at the root and context of a word, you may be able to figure out its meaning. Examining the roots of words is both a good way to increase your vocabulary and a fun exercise. And once you start, it becomes second nature.

SYNONYMS

A powerful way to increase your vocabulary is by learning synonyms for some common and frequently used words. Analyze your own vocabulary to see if you are using one or two words all the time. Then find some synonyms for these words and incorporate the new words into your vocabulary.

Take a look at the following commonly used words and some of their synonyms.

USING ROOT WORDS TO INCREASE YOUR VOCABULARY

Root	Meaning	Words
sta	to stay in one place	stationary obstacle stable
qui	quiet	quiet tranquil acquiesce
ver	truth	verdict veracious verify
vid/vis	to see	video television visionary
annu	year	annual anniversary biannual
eu	good	euphoria eulogy euphony
in	not	inactive inept insincere
mut	change	mutant commute mutation
phone	sound	telephone megaphone symphony
omni	all	omnipresent omnipotent omniscient
peri	around	peripheral periscope perimeter

USING SYNONYMS TO INCREASE YOUR VOCABULARY

WORD	SYNONYMS
said	spoke, uttered, voiced, stated
want	need, require
easy	simple, lenient
happy	blissful, joyful, gay
sad	somber, melancholy, morose
with	among, in the company of, in association
have	own, hold, possess
add	attach, affix
beginning	initial, origin
teach	instruct, train

Once you begin to integrate synonyms into your vocabulary, you will find that the process becomes easier and more entertaining. Use your thesaurus to find synonyms and watch your vocabulary increase.

SIMILAR WORDS

Many words in English sound very similar, and so people have a tendency to confuse both their pronunciation and meaning. Examine the words in the table on the next page to see if you or someone you know has been using them incorrectly.

Incorporating the preceding words and other similar sounding words can bring you one step closer to a more professional vocabulary.

Now review the information you have learned by completing the following exercises and quiz. Best of luck!

EXERCISES

A. Over the next two months, use the information in this chapter to learn at least one new word each week. After the two-month period, examine your progress, pat yourself on the back, and decide if you want to continue on the road to a more professional vocabulary.

B. Over the next two months, read a newspaper or magazine for at least 30 minutes each day. Pick out some unfamiliar words and follow the information from this chapter to determine their meanings.

SIMILAR WORDS

WORDS	MEANINGS
ac cede	to agree
ex ceed	to surpass
ac cess	passage, entry
ex cess	surplus, immoderation
a dapt	adjust, acclimate
a dept	skilled, competent
breadth	width
breath	inhale and exhale of air
im mi nent	looming, near
em i nent	distinguished, celebrated
in dig e nous	native to a place
in di gent	needy, poor
in ter state	between the states
in tra state	within a state
la ter	subsequent
lat ter	second of two things
light en ing	illuminated, brightening
light ning	massive discharge
per se cute	oppress
pro se cute	file suit in court
ve ra cious	truthful, honest
vo ra cious	greedy
wheth er	in any case
whith er	where

Quiz

1. What are some ways to increase your vocabulary?

Answer Key

1. Some ways to increase your vocabulary include the following:

   a. Use a dictionary and thesaurus faithfully.

b. Read periodicals like the *New York Times*, *Wall Street Journal*, and *U.S. News & World Report*.

c. Create mental pictures of words that are difficult and use flashcards.

d. Be patient and recognize that an effective vocabulary takes time to develop.

NEXT STEP

Congratulations for completing this chapter. Move on to the next chapter, *Handling Conflict at Work*, and continue along the road to becoming a more effective communicator!

CHAPTER 14

HANDLING CONFLICT AT WORK

There is no work situation that exists without some degree of conflict. As much as we may dream about a nurturing occupation without struggle, the truth is that there will always be some conflict.

It is true, however, that conflict at work can be beneficial. As a result of conflict, you can learn what your boss, colleague, customer, or even yourself really want in a certain situation. And conflict generally results in change that can be productive for everyone.

The main reason that most workers dislike conflict is because it can involve aggressiveness, defensiveness, or other negative emotional responses. But conflict doesn't have to be negative. If you apply rational and constructive guidelines to handling conflict situations, you can help eliminate negativity and increase productivity in your business.

In this chapter we'll discuss various ways to handle conflict at work. We'll discuss how to receive criticism, give criticism, control negative emotions, and deal with disappointment. First, let's look at how to receive criticism.

CRITICISM

If you haven't already encountered criticism at work, be grateful. On the other hand, if you have received what you consider to be more than enough criticism, join the club. At one time or another, everyone in the workplace receives his or her jolt of criticism. It could be from a customer who is upset about an incorrect bill, your boss who doesn't understand why you ordered the parts last week, or a colleague who thinks that you're stepping into his territory. Whatever the situation, criticism can hurt.

People say things like:

- "You're always upsetting everyone."
- "Why can't you ever get things right?"
- "You really messed up this job."
- "This mistake was unbelievably bad."

Comments like these can ruin your whole day, your week, or even the life of your job. The key to handling criticism is to control the way you react to it. The following list of guidelines will help you to turn negative criticism into a positive learning experience.

Receiving Criticism

One of the most important things we can do when receiving criticism is to *not* be defensive. When someone says something to us like, "The way you acted upset everyone at the meeting," we become justifiably upset. One of our first reactions is to try to protect ourselves. As a result we may respond with, "Oh yeah, you're the one who ruined the discussion" or "You think I upset everyone? Get a life."

When we say these things we're just trying to save face or preserve a positive image of ourselves. What we should try to do, however, is find out if there really is any truth in the criticism and if we need to change our behavior. While it certainly is not easy to practice nondefensiveness, it can be one of the most effective ways of responding to criticism.

The next time that you receive a stab of criticism, bite your tongue. Avoid the temptation to strike back at the other person. Decide that you will investigate the remark to see if it has any merit. Being nondefensive is extremely difficult, but it's particularly useful when dealing with a variety of people in the workplace.

Second, you need to seek more information from your critic. When your boss says, "You did not act in a professional manner," ask her exactly what she meant. Your response could be, "Would you be more specific in explaining why you think I was not professional?" Ask the question as rationally as you can, avoiding defensive nonverbal behavior like rolling your eyes, raising a finger in a defiant manner, or shaking your head back and forth.

If your critic can't think of anything specific to justify his or her comment, then you may want to suggest some interpretations. Comments like, "Did you think that I was too loud?" or "Would you like me to refrain from asking about Mr. Black's health?" may help you to understand the underlying reasons for the criticism.

There may be times when your critic doesn't say anything but you know there's something wrong. A colleague who pouts around the office or a boss who slams materials on the desk is probably trying to give you some nonverbal clues. In these situations, talk about what you observe. You could say something like, "Marge, I've noticed that you've been pacing around the office and you haven't said anything all morning. Is there something wrong?" or "Ms. Barless, I've observed that you've thrown your paperwork down on the desk. Is something bothering you?" Clarification of nonverbal behaviors will help office members to be more productive.

Third, you may want to paraphrase a critical remark so that you and the critic will have a better understanding of the problem. If you work in a department store and a customer says, "I can't believe this. I can't find anything. I've been searching and searching for clothes all by myself," you may want to respond with, "Would

REMINDERS FOR RECEIVING CRITICISM

1. Don't be defensive.
2. Seek more information. Ask for specifics.
3. Learn to paraphrase criticism.
4. Ask what your critic would like to happen as a result of the criticism.
5. Admit your mistakes.

WORDS FROM THE WISE

"The point that most needs to be borne in mind is that the welfare of every business is dependent upon cooperation and teamwork on the part of its personnel. Proper cooperation cannot be secured between groups of men who are constantly quarreling among themselves over petty grievances."

—*Charles Gow*

you like some assistance? I apologize that no one has offered to help you before this." Or if your boss states, "These disruptions at work must stop," you could reply by stating, "Are you saying that our interdepartmental coffee breaks are interfering with work?" The bottom line is that paraphrasing can help you figure out why the critic is upset.

Fourth, ask the critic what he or she wants you to do as a result of the criticism. If a colleague who sits next to you says, "Your fluorescent light is always shining on my terminal," you could ask if he'd like you to place the light in a different location. Or if your boss complains that the invoices are always late, ask him if he'd like to move the billing cycle up three days. An important, yet overlooked, aspect of criticism is that it can lead to changes that will create a win–win situation for everyone.

Fifth, if you know that you're wrong, admit it. When you know your office mate is right when she objects to your messy desk, agree with her and concentrate on changing your behavior. Or when your customer complains that she's been waiting five minutes while you've been on the phone, apologize and make every effort to create a positive experience for her.

Giving Criticism

Many times at work you'll need to offer constructive criticism to someone. Perhaps your coworker is continually late with his part of your project or five minutes before your work day is to end, your boss asks you to type a 10-page report. In these and many other similar situations you'll be responsible for providing feedback to improve the situation. While these situations can be difficult, they are manageable. Use the following guidelines to assist you in offering constructive criticism.

First, practice assertiveness. Being assertive involves standing up for yourself without hurting anyone else. If you don't like the fact that you're the only person who brings in coffee for the staff or that someone is always making fun of you, then you need to be assertive. These situations demand that you voice your opinion and state what is wrong.

Many people place others' feelings before their own needs and emotions. They want everyone to like them and will go to any extent not to alienate coworkers. A problem arises, however, when resentment builds because everyone else's needs and wants are considered first. This can lead to an emotional explosion or mounting stress. Therefore, it's important to make others aware of what you want.

Second, focus your feedback on the *behavior*, not the person. Rather than say that your coworker is unprofessional, you could say that wearing cut-offs and dirty tennis shoes to the boss's retirement party was unprofessional. Or, instead of accusing your supervisor of being sexist, you could reiterate her remark and explain why you think the statement was sexist.

Third, make sure that you have enough evidence to support criticism. There may be times when your coworker or employee does something out of character and it really doesn't affect your business or personnel. Give him or her the benefit of the doubt. Criticize only those behaviors that become a pattern and are detrimental to the company or an individual.

Fourth, provide the criticism as soon as you can after the behavior occurs. There's nothing worse than for someone to criticize an act that occurred months before. Most people have a difficult time remembering what happened the day before, not to mention three months prior to the criticism.

REMINDERS FOR GIVING CRITICISM

1. Practice assertiveness. No one gains at work if you are either nonassertive or aggressive.
2. Focus your feedback on the behavior, not the person. An *act* is unprofessional, not the person.
3. Make sure that you have enough evidence to support your criticism.
4. Give criticism as soon as you can after the act occurs.
5. Make sure you offer feedback in a neutral situation.
6. Listen carefully to what the other person says. There is a chance that you have misinterpreted her behavior.
7. Go into a confrontation with an objective to solve, not perpetuate, a problem.

Fifth, make sure that the situation and time are right for offering criticism. Giving feedback at a team meeting or one day before a coworker goes in for surgery is not a good idea. Make sure that both you and the other person can discuss the feedback as rationally as possible in a neutral climate.

Sixth, listen carefully to what the other person says. Let him or her do the talking. You may have interpreted a situation incorrectly. If your coworker is not completing her work on time, you may find out that there is an unequal distribution of assignments. Perhaps she has too much work to do and needs a lighter work load.

Finally, go into every conflict situation with an objective to learn something and solve, not perpetuate, the problem. Look for a solution that would benefit all parties. If you're upset because you always have to stay late to take notes at a board meeting, perhaps you could suggest that you come in later in the morning on board days. Or if something your coworker says is troubling you, give her an opportunity to air her complaints too. The point is that you want to resolve any conflict and strive to make things better.

ELIMINATING INTERRUPTIONS

Many times at work someone will interrupt your train of thought while you're working on a project. Or you'll be right in the middle of explaining your idea when a colleague asks an unrelated question. Unless you have a personal secretary who will screen your calls and visits, then you need to learn how to handle interruptions. Look over the following guidelines for eliminating interruptions.

First, practice your assertive skills. If a coworker is always coming to your office to discuss his weight-loss program, don't wait until he's lost 50 pounds. Let

REMINDERS FOR ELIMINATING INTERUPTIONS

1. Be assertive. Don't let interruptions build to the point where they're a problem.
2. Have a secretary, coworker, or answering machine screen your calls. Let callers know when to call back or when you'll be returning calls.
3. Use final cues on the telephone to indicate that the conversation is ending.
4. Use assertive skills to squelch an interruption.
5. During a formal public speech, let the audience know that there will be a question-and-answer period at the end of your talk.

him know that you are really busy and that you could discuss his progress over a nonfat lunch or after work. If you have a private office, close your door when you must concentrate. By practicing assertiveness, you can stop a potential problem from escalating.

Second, if it's possible, ask a secretary or colleague to screen disruptive telephone calls. Another option might be to use an answering machine to screen interruptions. It should be clear to the caller that you will return calls the same day during a designated time period. If you have a secretary or coworker answering for you, callers can be asked if it's an emergency and you need to be interrupted.

Third, use final cues on the phone to indicate that the conversation is coming to a close. You can say things like, "Before we hang up, I'd just like to thank you for your hard work," or "I'll let you get back to your work." Final cues provide the subtle yet assertive tips that you need to conclude the conversation.

Fourth, if someone interrupts you at a business meeting, there are two ways to handle the situation. When an interruption occurs, you could continue talking in a louder voice. You could maintain eye contact with the person to whom you were talking and give the interrupter a nonverbal cue, such as a raised hand to indicate that he should stop. Or you could state that you have not completed your ideas. A simple, "Greg, let me finish my train of thought," should end the interruption. The most imporant thing is to stop people from interrupting you. If you set a precedent of letting someone interrupt you, the problem will only continue.

Fifth, whenever you're speaking to a large group of people in a more formal public speaking situation, you may have to establish that a question-and-answer period will follow your talk. Most people recognize that this is the protocol when someone is speaking in front of a group, but there may be a situation when you need to say, "I'll be answering questions at the end of my speech."

By practicing these guidelines you should be able to keep interruptions to a minimum.

NEGATIVE EMOTIONS

Many times at work negative emotions may interfere with your activities. A crisis at home or on the way to work can ruin your day and decrease your productivity. You may be upset because you know that you've made a mistake or hurt someone's feelings. Or perhaps you're concerned that you'll be part of the group that receives pink slips.

Whatever the case, there will be a time when negative emotions will take over your rational thoughts and decrease your productivity. You should however, work to eliminate contrary thinking that does nothing for you or your business. Research demonstrates that worry, anger, or other negative emotions can jeopardize your ability to be an efficient worker. So, read over the following guidelines and strive to eliminate negative emotions from your workplace.

Eliminating Negative Emotions

First and foremost, remember that you are responsible for how you feel. As the commander of your ship, you and you alone have the power to change the way you feel. You can choose to be positive or negative at work. No one can make you feel humiliated or rejected without your permission. By maintaining a calm and positive demeanor, you can take a rational look at your feelings and strive to solve the problem.

Second, as an old and wise adage states, "Don't cry over spilled milk." If you make a mistake, correct it, apologize, and try to never let it happen again. But don't beat yourself up over and over. Life is a learning experience for everyone. Once we truly accept that our whole life is a learning experience, we can concentrate on our growth. Remember, there is nothing you can do to undo a mistake. So let it go and learn from it.

Third, there may be a negative situation coming up that is out of your control. Maybe your boss has decided that you should work with someone you dislike. Or perhaps you'll have to work overtime on the busiest day of the year. What is important is that you realize that there are certain things in life that are out of your control. The test of life is to accept what will happen and make the best of the situation. As another old adage so aptly states, "When life hands you lemons, make lemonade."

REMINDERS FOR ELIMINATING NEGATIVE EMOTIONS

1. Recognize that you are responsible for how you feel. Choose to be positive and react to situations in a calm and rational manner.
2. Don't cry over spilled milk.
3. When life gives you lemons, make lemonade.
4. Never take out your anger on someone else.
5. Think before you react to a situation.
6. Recognize that positive feelings have a positive result on your work performance.

WORDS FROM THE WISE

" 'Tis a fundamental rule of life that unless you rule yourself
you will be mercilessly ruled by others."

—*Thomas Blandi*

Fourth, never take your negative emotions out on someone else. Recognize that you are an adult and that angry remarks or a threatening tone are not even acceptable from children. A mature worker doesn't snap at someone else because of what happened to her.

Fifth, when a negative situation occurs, take your time to figure out how you will react. Too many times the impulsive act is the wrong one, so think before you respond to a negative situation.

Sixth, accept the truth that negative emotions can have a debilitating effect on your performance. Keep busy at work and don't let worry, anger, or negativity have a chance to decrease your abilities.

Once you have incorporated these guidelines into your work habits, you will reap the benefits of stronger self-control and more productivity.

By incorporating the guidelines from this chapter into your work habits, you will be one step closer to becoming a more effective worker. Now review this chapter's concepts by completing the following exercises and questions.

EXERCISES

A. The next time you receive negative feedback, use the guidelines on receiving criticism. Keep a written account of when you received the criticism, who spoke to you, and your response. Look over your document periodically to see if you need to change some behaviors. Remember to look at criticism as an opportunity to grow.

B. Practice assertiveness at work. When you think that you are being taken advantage of, speak up. Remember that if you don't take care of yourself, no one will.

Quiz

1. What are some guidelines for receiving criticism?
2. What are some guidelines for giving criticism?

3. What can you do to eliminate bothersome interruptions?

4. How can you handle negative emotions?

Answer Key

1. When you receive criticism:
    a. Avoid defensiveness.
    b. Seek specific information.
    c. Paraphrase the criticism if necessary.
    d. Ask what the critic wants you to do as a result of the criticism.
    e. Admit your mistakes.
2. When you offer criticism:
    a. Practice assertiveness.
    b. Focus on the behavior, not the person.
    c. Support your criticism with evidence.
    d. Offer criticism immediately after the behavior occurs.
    e. Offer criticism in a neutral environment.
    f. Listen carefully to what the other person says.
    g. Work to solve, not perpetuate a problem.
3. To eliminate interruptions:
    a. Stop the interruptions before they become a serious problem.
    b. Have someone or an answering device screen your calls.
    c. Use final cues to let a caller know that the conversation is ending.
    d. Use assertive skills to squelch interruptions.
    e. During a speech, let the audience know that questions will be answered after the speech.
4. Follow these guidelines to eliminate negative emotions at work:
    a. Recognize that you are responsible for how you feel.
    b. Don't cry over spilled milk.
    c. When given lemons, try to make lemonade.
    d. Never take your anger out on someone else.
    e. Think before you react to the situation.
    f. Recognize that positive thoughts have a positive impact on your work.

NEXT STEP

Once again you've completed another chapter. Great work! Now move on to Chapter 15, *Meetings That Pay Off.*

HAPTER | 15

MEETINGS THAT PAY OFF

Many employees attend meetings and wonder why they're there. Some businesses establish weekly meetings and neglect to inform participants what the purpose of the meetings are. Thousands of managers who spend 30% of their time in charge of meetings have no idea how to run an effective one. And innumerable meetings are ended with no summary of what future responsibilities for meeting participants will be.

All of these common problems are most disturbing when you consider that business meetings are a major investment of time and money. And as we know, businesses are not supposed to operate with a loss of either time or money!

There are, however, some specific guidelines to follow for increasing the productivity of business meetings. We'll cover these helpful tips by examining the purposes for meetings and the responsibilities for both leaders and participants. First, let's take a look at why we should have meetings.

PURPOSES OF MEETINGS

The most common reasons to hold a meeting include to inform, to strategize, to motivate, and to brainstorm. Some meetings have multiple purposes, but there is generally one primary reason that people are coming together. Let's examine these purposes.

The majority of meetings are held so that information can be exchanged. Your business may have a meeting where departmental heads provide an update on the latest occurrences in their areas. Or your department may have its own meeting where individuals share their projects. There may be an annual meeting where shareholders are informed about their holdings. The task in an informative meeting is to "spread the word" in a clear and concise manner. Most businesses establish an official organizational structure that enables information to be disseminated through meetings in an effective manner.

At the second type of meeting, a strategy meeting, members are faced with a problem that they must cooperatively solve. For example, when faced with a sales quota, sales personnel may come together to create an effective plan for achieving the goal. Or when there are complaints, customer service representatives may meet to solve the problem.

Motivational meetings take place so that businesses can improve employees' morale. There may be a meeting at the beginning of the year to "kick off" a new period. Or a business may hold a meeting after a project is completed so that all employees can get psyched about the new project. Motivational meetings provide rejuvenation or incentive to keep employees enthusiastic about their positions.

The meeting to brainstorm is generally used in artistic and creative businesses. In an advertising agency, you may have the creative staff meet to identify a new slogan, logo, or look for a product. A public relations firm may hold a meeting to brainstorm about the type of image a client should project. Brainstorming enables people to feed off each other, generating spontaneous ideas that eventually result in effective and collective ideas.

Whether your business sponsors a meeting to inform, strategize, motivate, or brainstorm, there are two major components that every effective meeting must satisfy. Let's examine these components.

Two Components of a Meeting

The most important ingredient of an effective meeting is a reason to meet. This may sound simple and obvious, but many meetings are held just because they're

WORDS FROM THE WISE

"The strength of an organization is not I. It is we."

—*A. B. Zu Tavern*

on the schedule. Participants may walk away from a meeting with little or no new information or instruction. You need to make sure that there is a purpose for the meeting and that all the participants are clear about that purpose.

When you define the purpose of your meeting, make sure that a meeting is the simplest or cheapest way to achieve your objective. Perhaps it would be more cost-effective to send out a report and ask for comments or to meet with employees on a one-to-one basis. It is crucial for productivity and employee morale to have a specific objective and to know that a meeting is the best way to accomplish that objective.

The second component for effective meetings involves being a team player. It involves developing a respectful and cooperative attitude. Even if you don't agree with someone, you must still respect his or her right to voice their opinions and ideas on a topic. Each member must also accept the fact that many times his or her point of view may not become the guiding force for a group. Being respectful and cooperative will eliminate negative emotions that can otherwise occur in a meeting.

LEADERSHIP STYLES

Leadership styles can vary slightly according to situation and group composition, but most people rule in one of three ways. The most controlling style is referred to as *autocratic*. An autocratic leader calls all the shots, delegating specific tasks, and asking for very little, if any, input from other participants. The autocratic leader truly believes that he or she has the best, and many times, only profitable and effective ideas.

This type of leadership may result in immediate decisions but is deficient in individual morale support and team building. Autocratic leadership is essential in situations such as war. Can you imagine a war situation where a general asks his troops if they want to pick up their rifles and fight? Or a schoolroom where the teacher asks a child if he's ready to stop biting? In certain situations, the autocratic style must be used.

On the other end of the spectrum, the *laissez-faire* leader is virtually no leader at all. All the ideas come from participants, and responsibilities are most certainly assigned to other members. Some creative ideas may occur in this style, but generally members feel like they're in a boat without a rudder. Employees get frustrated, and time and money are wasted.

The *democratic* style is the favored form of leadership. The democratic leader is supportive of and interested in participants' input. A democratic leader will strive to be fair and listen to everyone, while at the same time directing participants toward a specific objective. To solve a problem, the democratic leader asks more questions, whereas the autocratic leader issues orders. The democratic leader uses feedback from other members to make final decisions. The democratic style can result in longer meetings, but it generally results in more involved and satisfied employees. In fact, sociologists have concluded that the best leaders are sensitive to the interests of all group members, enabling each individual to participate actively.

Leadership Responsibilities

Being the leader of a meeting is no easy task. It involves work before, during, and after the meeting. The following list of responsibilities will help you to assume an effective leadership role when conducting business meetings.

First, state the purpose of the meeting. The best thing to do is to disseminate an agenda and any pertinent information before the actual meeting. This gives your participants some time to prepare for the meeting. The more informed and encouraged to prepare your participants are prior to the meeting, the more insightful and beneficial their input will be.

Second, create an environment that is as conducive to productivity as you can make it. This means that you must consider the seating, lighting, external noise, and refreshments.

If you're looking for maximum interaction among participants, a circular table works best. People can see each other better, and it's a democratic arrangement for seating. Because most businesses have only rectangular tables, then you will most likely have to work with it.

Make sure that you have the correct number of chairs. Too many chairs means that at least two people will have a chair in between them. This limits interaction, so take a count of attendees and plan appropriately.

Always check out your conference or meeting room before your meeting. There may be external noises like a humming flourescent light that should be taken care of before you meet.

REMINDERS FOR EFFECTIVE LEADERSHIP

1. Make sure that everyone knows why you're meeting. Be responsible for an announcement, agenda, and minutes.
2. Plan for a suitable environment.
3. Begin the meeting by introducing new members, reviewing the purpose, and referring to the agenda.
4. Keep the meeting moving.
5. Be prepared to handle any conflict that may arise.
6. Praise participants.
7. At the end of a meeting, summarize the decisions and plans, review individuals' tasks, and thank members for their involvement.

If you're responsible for refreshments, find out what is usually served and order those items. A combination of nerves and talking can contribute to a dry mouth, so at the very least, make sure that water is available. And if there are any other items (paper, pens, notepads, etc.) that are necessary, don't neglect your duty.

Before the meeting, make sure that the room is clean and the temperature is appropriate. Researchers agree that an ideal temperature for productivity is about 70 degrees.

You could add an individual touch to the meeting room by adding a vase of flowers or a plant. You might brighten someone's day and increase the group's creative approach to problems.

Third, when the meeting begins (and it must begin on time), introduce new members, review the purpose, and refer to the agenda. As you move through each item on the agenda, adhere to a preconceived time line so that you'll complete the meeting on time.

Fourth, during a meeting, keep the discussion going by asking questions, paraphrasing unclear comments, and providing background information that some participants may not have. It is also the leader's responsibility to bring participants who digress back to the topic under consideration.

Fifth, a leader must be able to handle any conflicts. A leader must be ready to step in and resolve any misunderstandings that may develop. Conflict resolution involves listening carefully to what participants are saying, being rational, and taking command of any disruptions.

Sixth, throughout the meeting, a leader needs to praise each individual's efforts and never embarrass anyone. Give people the opportunity to save face.

WORDS FROM THE WISE

"Few leaders are born leaders. Leadership is achieved by ability, alertness, experience, and keeping posted; by willingness to accept responsibility; a knack for getting along with people; an open mind and a head that stays clear under stress."

—*E. F. Girard*

"Leadership always requires a very thorough knowledge of the job. If a man does not understand the work he is undertaking to direct, naturally he cannot be expected to be a good leader."

—*Charles Gow*

Finally, at the end of a meeting, a leader needs to summarize the group's major decisions or plans, review the assignment of tasks, and genuinely be appreciative of the time and energy expended by each member.

After the meeting, a leader needs to make sure that minutes are disseminated as soon as possible and that participants are completing their assigned tasks.

Coordinating and leading a meeting can be a challenge, so plan ahead and follow these reminders for effective leadership:

WRITTEN MATERIALS FOR A MEETING

As the leader of a meeting, you are responsible for three written documents for every meeting. These include an announcement, agenda, and minutes. Let's take a closer look at each of these materials.

Announcement of a Meeting

It is the responsibility of the leader to disseminate an announcement of an upcoming meeting. Each member of the meeting should receive an announcement with adequate time to prepare. The most important aspects of an announcement include the subject, date, time, place, and responsibilities of the participants. Supplementary materials should include a copy of the agenda, letters, reports, or any additional materials that must be examined before the meeting. An announcement should look like the following:

TO: All Members of the Sales Department at Sabino
FROM: Jesse
SUBJECT: Sales Meeting
                Thursday, January 16, 1999
                10:00 a.m., Suite 333
DATE: January 2, 1999

It is imperative that all members of our sales department attend
the meeting on January 16. We will review every facet of
our new project, SalesPlus.

Come to the meeting prepared to discuss your projected budget
for the next year, specific objectives of your team, and requests
for any ways the group can assist you in achieving your goals.

Please RSVP to my assistant, Annie Mack, at ext. 432.
Let her know if you need any assistance in copying your
materials or setting up visual aids.

Thanks in advance for making our new project a success!

An Agenda

An agenda is a plan for a meeting. It is a written document that lists what will be
discussed at a meeting and in what order items will be covered. An agenda is an
important part of keeping a meeting focused. An agenda should include the date,
place, and time of the meeting as well as the topics that will be covered. The
agenda needs to be sent out with the announcement. An agenda should look like
the following:

Agenda for Sabino Sales Meeting

January 13, 1999

Suite 333

I.   Opening and Introductions   John
II.   Last Year's Project   Beth

III.	Team 1's Update	Vera
IV.	Team 2's Update	Leslie
V.	Team 3's Update	Frank
VI.	Team 4's Update	Casey
VII.	Budget	Pat
VIII.	Assignments and Wrap-Up	John

Minutes

In addition to following up on participants' completion of assignments after a meeting, you need to disseminate minutes. Minutes will remind members of their responsibilities as well as provide an overall picture of what occurred. An excerpt of a meeting's minutes follows:

Minutes of Sabino Sales

January 13, 1999

Suite 333

Present: John M., Beth G., Vera W., Leslie M., Casey M., Pat C., Margaret S., Nancy Z., Tom G., Anne P., and Linda N.

I. John welcomed the sales staff and complimented them for their fine work. Vera recommended that Wayne Black, Sabino President, be invited to the next meeting. John will invite Wayne to the next meeting.
Due: February 1

II. Beth distributed Team 1's objectives for SalesPlus plan. Leslie suggested that Sahuaro Businessses be included in the outreach portion. Beth will follow through with this recommendation and submit a formal budget to John.
Due: January 20, 1999

III. Vera displayed a flowchart of Team 2's organization. John requested that copies be made for all sales staff.
Due: January 15, 1999

IV. Leslie disucussed Team 3's three-part strategy and requested clerical assistance to carry out the plan. John approved a part-time temporary assistant to be hired as soon as possible.
Due: February 1, 1999

Respectfully Submitted,
Annie Mack
Recording Secretary and John's Assistant

BEING A PARTICIPANT

A lot of people think that when you attend a meeting, your only responsibility is to fill a seat. Can you imagine if everyone attended meetings with that same philosophy? You'd have 10 passive observers and one speaker. And there would be serious concerns about the effectiveness of the meeting.

As a participant, you need to be prepared, organized, curious, analytical, and cooperative. Some people feel that speaking to a group of their coworkers is more difficult than speaking to a large group of strangers. This is because they feel like the rewards and costs are greater as they are around these people all the time.

However you feel about your attendance at a meeting, bite the bullet and learn to contribute fully at every meeting. To be the most productive participant you can be, follow these tips for being a responsible member of a meeting.

Responsibilities of a Participant

First, always be prepared. Know the purpose of your meeting. If the leader of the meeting doesn't tell you, ask for more information. Do your homework. Read and think about handouts and prepare any necessary written materials. Your professional credibility may be riding on your performance at a meeting.

Second, always sit in a strategic spot at the meeting. Research indicates that we talk most to people we can see and hear, so you may want to sit across from the leader of the group. Sitting in a key position will result in more chances to be heard.

Third, avoid lengthy speeches. It's always a good idea to be brief. Make your point in four or five sentences. Then support your point with one documented reason. You can always add additional evidence later. You'll find that simplicity pays off.

Fourth, listen, be flexible, and stay alert. Meetings are full of interruptions, new ideas, and spontaneous requests. Don't be caught daydreaming when you should be actively involved in the meeting.

Fifth, focus your comments on the topic at hand. You may have an unrelated yet fascinating point to make, but avoid the temptation to discuss it. Most employees at a business meeting want to get back to their other work and are irritated when someone spends time on an aside.

Sixth, use evidence to support your points. People will be persuaded if you back up your "I think" statements with facts, statistics, and quotations so incorporate them into your reasoning.

Seventh, always assist, not alienate, your leader. If there is a misunderstanding among members of the group that only you understand, facilitate the rest of the group's comprehension. For example, you might say, "I believe Mark is referring to last week's complaint from Spitzer Industries that our deliveries are always two days late."

Eighth, point out other members' positive remarks and disagree in a rational, nonjudgmental manner. Comments such as, "I agree with Heather's statement. We should increase our telephone budget. And based on the 20% increase of telephone calls we've made over the past two months, it's important that we make this change immediately."

Or to disagree you might say, "John's point does have some obvious merit. I do, however, disagree with his overall plan. Let me briefly explain our department's three-point plan which includes John's ideas."

Finally, as with any oral communication, watch your posture (don't slouch), speak slowly and clearly, be attentive, and display interest and enthusiasm. It is extremely important that participants at your meeting believe that you care about the business.

CHECKLIST OF PARTICIPANT RESPONSIBILITIES

✔ Always be prepared.
✔ Sit in a strategic position.
✔ Be brief.
✔ Listen, be flexible, and stay alert.
✔ Stay focused on the subject.
✔ Use evidence to support your "I think" statements.
✔ Assist the leader.
✔ Reinforce other members and practice rational disagreement.
✔ Watch your verbal and nonverbal communication.

WORDS FROM THE WISE

"Men are judged to a large degree by their ability to work with other men."

—*Robert F. Black*

Congratulations on the completion of this material. Now it's time to complete the exercises and quiz. If you need to, you can refer back to material in this chapter.

EXERCISE

A. Attend a meeting at work with an analytical eye. Analyze the meeting according to the following criteria:
 1. Was the purpose clear?
 2. What leadership style was used?
 3. What made the leader effective or ineffective?
 4. Which member contributed the most? What did he or she do?
 5. Which member contributed the least? What did he or she do?

Quiz

1. What are two essential components for an effective meeting?
2. What are three leadership styles?
3. List five responsibilities for an effective leader.
4. List five responsibilities for an effective participant.
5. What are the three written materials that must accompany any meeting?

Answer Key

1. Two essential components of a meeting involve:
   a. defining the purpose of the meeting and
   b. working as a team
2. Three types of leadership styles are the following:
   a. autocratic
   b. laissez-faire and
   c. democratic
3. A leader's responsibilities are the following:
   a. defining the purpose of the meeting

    b. organizing written materials

    c. keeping the meeting moving and focused

    d. handling conflict

    e. summarizing decisions, and participants' tasks and following through to make sure that everything is accomplished

4. A meeting's written materials include the following:

    a. announcement

    b. agenda

    c. minutes

5. Meeting participants need to do the following:

    a. be prepared

    b. be brief

    c. listen

    d. stay focused

    e. use evidence

NEXT STEP

Another job well done! Continue to Chapter 16, *Telephone Skills*, and keep up the good work!

TELEPHONE SKILLS

Today there are more than one billion telephones in the world. Each minute, thousands of business transactions occur over the telephone. Employees spend three times as much time talking on the telephone as they do using any other technology. And executives spend approximately 14% of their time on the phone.

Rather than taking the time to write a letter, send an e-mail, or meet with someone in person, most customers want to conduct business as quickly as possible. And that means that more and more transactions are being conducted over the telephone.

Telephone conversations in business should be quick with an immediate response. Clients should be able to solve in a few minutes a problem that could take up to two weeks by letter. People call about things like orders, billing, sales, and complaints. The way you treat these customers will determine whether they return to your business.

Being courteous and professional is particularly important on the telephone, as you may be the only contact a person has with your company. Telephone skills require excellent oral communication abilities that will keep your customers coming back. Whether you answer the phone on a permanent or occasional basis, you'll need to be aware of your business's telephone equipment, procedures for calling other people, and practices of successful telephone receptionists. First, let's discuss the variety of telephone equipment and operations that are available today.

TELEPHONE EQUIPMENT

Whether you are answering your business line for the first time or the 100th time, you should be aware of employees' numbers and extensions, where you need to route specific concerns and questions, and the capabilities of your phone lines. The numbers, extensions, and routing procedures are determined at each business. The capabilities of a business's phone system vary according to the type and number of calls a business receives. Here's an overview of some of the basic business devices for your telephone lines.

Basic Telephone Functions

Data lines: The capability to transmit more than sound on your telephone line. Businesses can send data such as video or facsimile (fax) anywhere in the world. You can have a separate line for your fax or share a line with your telephone.

Priority call: Important customers may receive a special ring on your phone line.

Three-way conferencing: Your phone can enable people at three or more locations to talk simultaneously.

800 service line: With a special 800 or 888 number, your customers will be able to call you free of charge.

Automatic call sequencer: Your business calls will be answered by a recorded message. Caller holds for the first available person.

Cellular mobile phone: Mobile phone that can be used in a car or from a distance location.

Videoconferencing: Enables a conference with both audio and video capabilities to take place via phone line.

Speed dial: Stores important customers' phone numbers so that you can push a button to dial them quickly.

Redial: Redial retries your call when you get a busy signal the first time. It frees you from spending unnecessary time dialing a number over and over.

Special attachments for handicapped people: Special telephone equipment enables the handicapped to use the lines.

The bottom line in using your business line is to find out the capabilities of your phone. Know how to use each of these capabilities before you begin answering the phones. Remember, you may be the only contact a customer has with your business, and you want the interaction to be a positive one.

TELEPHONE CALLS

There will be many times when you are responsible for making an important business call. You could be calling to explain a bill, order parts, schedule a meeting, or any one of thousands of other reasons. There are several tried and true reminders to help you to make the most of your business calls. Let's take a look at each of them.

Tips for Calling

First, include an introduction in your telephone call. Include an enthusiastic greeting of "Hello," "Good morning," "Good afternoon," "Good evening," or, if it's okay with your boss, "Hi." Let them know who you are (Joseph Cottontail) and who you represent (Southwest Carrot Distributors). This introduction will help to establish rapport.

Second, know the specific purpose of your call and with whom you need to speak. Why and for whom are you making the call? Do you need to talk with a specific person or will anyone in a specific department be able to address you comments or questions?

Third, when you are talking to the correct person, politely state the purpose of your call. Are you calling to cancel the person's cable TV or to offer them a job? What do you want the outcome of your conversation to be? Try to state the purpose in "you" terms. Instead of saying, "We want your business, so sign up for this credit card," you would say, "You have the opportunity to receive this credit card." Just be careful not to overdo the "you" concept by using it excessively.

Fourth, before you actually make the call, write down any questions or comments that you absolutely must ask or make. Then when you're talking, look at your comments so that you cover everything. Also make sure that you have a pen and paper handy while you're on the phone. You may need to write down something important during the conversation.

REMINDERS FOR TELEPHONE CALLING

1. Begin your conversation by introducing who you are and whom you represent.
2. Know the specific purpose of your call and whom you need to contact.
3. Clearly state the purpose in "you" terms.
4. Have written notes available in addition to something to record information.
5. Really listen to the other person. And never interrupt.
6. Review the bottom line as a result of this conversation.

Fifth, use your best listening skills to understand the other person's perspective. And never, never interrupt.

At the end of the conversation, go over the bottom line. Review when or where you need the order, the address, or the agreements you made. A simple "Good. I'm glad you were able to decide that Emco will be responsible for the 500 missing staplers. You can send payment at your own convenience." This type of summary will keep both the caller and receiver abreast of the major decisions.

Answering the Telephone

One of the most important aspects of answering the telephone is to answer it promptly. If our call isn't answered after about three rings, we all get a bit irritable. Also keep the number of transfers to a minimum. Callers hate to be passed around until they just happen to be connected to the right person. If you can, stay with the caller until you do connect with the person they need to contact.

Second, always be positive. You're not being paid to be negative or aggressive toward your customers. Nor should you be cold and indifferent. Customers are attracted to a warm and interested voice, so listen and think about the image you are projecting. It always helps to record your voice (with someone else's permission, of course) during a conversation. Play it back and decide on any improvements you need to make.

Third, be prepared and never assume anything. Know where to find your forms, schedules, and extensions. Keep everything current and be prepared to write down any important information. When you give directions or instructions, start from the beginning. Don't assume that the caller already knows to turn left or right out of the driveway. It's easy for an instruction or direction to be miscommunicated because one step was left out.

Fourth, answer the phone in three parts. First give a greeting, like, "Good morning." Then state your business's name or office followed by "May I help you?" Your introductions would sound like these:

"Good afternoon. You've reached Western Clothes. How may I direct your call?"

"Hello. This is Marc Smithe's office. I'm Valerie. May I help you?"

"Good morning and welcome to Best Steaks. May I be of some assistance?"

There's a fine line between giving a caller too much and not enough information. Generally, however, it's best not to overload someone with too much information so that you can find out why they're calling.

If a caller asks who you are or what your title is, tell them. Never say, "Oh, I'm just an administrative assistant." Be proud of whatever work you do and don't degrade yourself.

Fifth, if you must screen calls, do it in a professional manner. Today more than ever before, customers are becoming savvy about business calls. If an assistant asks for a name, places the caller on hold for one minute, and returns to say that Mr. Wiles stepped out of the office, most people are aware that the person they're calling doesn't want to talk to them.

If you can, never screen calls or create a sophisticated system for screening without a caller's knowledge. You never want to alienate a customer, so practice courteous and nondiscriminatory behavior.

Sixth, always write down a message. Never depend on your memory. To make the job easier, you can purchase a telephone pad at a business supply store. Or, if you're writing out the information, record the date and time, the caller and caller's telephone number, who the message is for, and any other message or additional information.

Seventh, as in all communication situations, listen to what the caller has to say. It's important to stay focused on what the other person is saying, not what you're going to have for lunch.

Eighth, never eat, drink, or chew on the telephone. You may think others can't tell what you have in your mouth, but they always can. It just is not professional to listen to someone eating on the phone.

REMINDERS FOR ANSWERING A CALL

1. Be prompt. Answer the phone immediately. Three rings is the limit a person should have to wait.
2. Be positive. Who wants to talk to a grump or an uninterested party?
3. Be prepared. Know everything you need to know about the phones, schedules, orders, or any other important information. The more you know, the better.
4. Greet the person, state your business's name or office, and offer to help the caller.
5. If you must screen calls, do it in a professional way.
6. Write down all important information.
7. Listen intently to what the caller has to say.
8. Never eat, drink, or chew on the telephone.
9. Summarize the conversation, thank the caller by name, and say good-bye.

Finally, end your conversation with a summary of the conversation, a thank you, good-bye, and the person's name. "Bye bye" is cute, but not professional for a business call.

Selling Over the Phone

In addition to the previous reminders for calling and receiving telephone calls, a salesperson should incorporate the following tips into their interactions on the phone.

First, when you receive an inquiry call about a product or service, get a complete description of what a caller wants. Some people know exactly what they want; some callers, however, are unaware of the choices available to them. It's your responsibility to ask questions to determine what they want to buy. You want satisfied customers so do your best to fill their needs and wants.

Second, be conversational and specific. Rather than say, "We deliver our orders fast," say, "We guarantee delivery within 24 hours." Give your caller just as much information as they need. The more you tell your customers about the benefits and options of a product or service, the more apt they are to find a reason to purchase what you're selling.

REMINDERS FOR SALES CALLS

1. Question your caller to find out what he or she really wants.
2. Be conversational and specific.
3. Be able to respond to an objection.
4. Leave a lasting positive impression.

Third, anticipate any objections to your product or service by having a response ready. If price appears to be an obstacle to purchasing your product, know the benefits of spending a bit more money. Do you have a warranty on your product? Does your service come with any additional benefits? Be ready to answer objections in a rational and positive manner.

Fourth, leave a positive impression. Always conclude a call with, "Thanks for calling," "If you have any concerns, give me a call," or "We appreciate your business." Make sure that your concluding remarks are genuine and straightforward. In addition, let your caller hang up first. You don't want to cut her off just when she's decided to make the purchase.

Following these sales call reminders will help you and your business.

ANSWERING MACHINES

Have you ever left a message on an answering machine and thought, "Did I remember to include the amount of cards we'll need?" Or have you spent too much time recording the message for your office? If you have, you're not alone. We've all wondered at one time or another if what we meant to say was really what we said.

The proliferation and accepted use of answering machines has changed the way we do business. The following list will enable you to achieve a professional manner when dealing with answering machine.

Use a Professional Manner

First, when you're leaving an outgoing message, keep it short and simple. Let people know what business they've reached, your business hours, and what information you want them to leave as a message. Do you want their name, number, and comments?

REMINDERS FOR USING ANSWERING MACHINE

1. Keep your outgoing message short and simple.
2. Avoid being funny, as it rarely works.
3. Update your message. There's nothing worse than hearing about a great sale after it's happened.
4. Write out the message and rehearse it before you read it.
5. When you're calling someone, be ready to leave a message. Get in the habit of writing things out so you'll cover everything.
6. Think about how you sound. If you're angry or frustrated, you may come across that way on the recording.

Second, avoid trying to be funny. What seems hilarious to you may seem unprofessional and odd to a customer. The Jack Nicholson sound-alike is inappropriate for a business recording.

Third, listen to your message and change your message when you need to. If your hours change or a special deal is available, you may want to change the recording. If your voice doesn't sound right, ask someone else to record the message.

Fourth, when recording your message, have everything written out so there can be no mistakes. Rehearse the message a few times before you deliver it into the phone. And if you're recording your message into the phone, your mouth should be approximately two inches away.

Fifth, when you're calling someone else, always be prepared to leave a message. Be ready with the list of information that you must leave on the answering machine. Be specific in your instructions. Include the times you can be reached or the date that you need to have the order filled. It's a good idea to leave your telephone number at the beginning and end of your message. Specificity will speed up your business transaction.

Sixth, think about how you sound. If you're overly frustrated or angry on the answering machine, you may regret it later. So, once again, be aware of how you're coming across.

Incorporating these six tips will help you to become more professional in the use of your telephone equipment.

Effective telephone skills are a must in business today. Incorporate the tips from this chapter into your communication and watch your confidence and business expertise soar. Now complete the following exercises and questions.

EXERCISES

A. Record your telephone conversation with someone. Analyze the impression you are making. What could you improve about your telephone skills? Write down the area you want to work on and make a concerted effort to improve your ability on the phone.

B. Listen carefully to other businesspeople calling you. Get in the habit of analyzing their telephone skills. What should be improved? Is there something about their skills that you would like to replicate? If so, strive to incorporate these positives into your telephone skills.

Quiz

1. What are some tips for making business calls?
2. How should you answer your business calls?
3. What will help you to improve your business image when using an answering machine?

Answer Key

1. When you make a business call, apply these tips:
   a. Give a complete introduction for yourself.
   b. Be specific about whom you want to speak to and why you're calling.
   c. State your purpose in "you" terms.
   d. Have written notes and a place to take notes.
   e. Listen to the other person. Never interrupt.
   f. Review the bottom line of any conversation.
2. When answering a business call, remember to do the following:
   a. Be prompt.
   b. Be positive.
   c. Be ready for any question or comment.
   d. Greet the person in three parts.
   e. Screen calls in a professional manner.
   f. Write down all important information.
   g. Listen to the caller.
   h. Never eat, drink, or chew gum on the phone.
   i. Summarize the important details.
3. When using an answering machine, remember to do the following:
   a. Keep your message short and simple.

b. Avoid being a comedian.

c. Update your messages.

d. Write out the message and rehearse it before you read it.

e. When you call someone, be thoroughly prepared to leave a message.

f. Avoid leaving a negative message.

NEXT STEP

Great work! You're moving right along! Now move on to the next chapter, *Successful Workshops.*

CHAPTER 17

SUCCESSFUL WORKSHOPS

Most people agree that "variety is the spice of life." This attitude is one of the reasons that workers in America should look forward to a seminar, training program, or workshop. These educational sessions should provide employees with an opportunity to break out of their work routine, learn something new, and have the opportunity to interact in a different environment.

It has been estimated that more than $60 billion is spent by American organizations each year to train and educate their employees. At some time during their work life, almost all employees will attend a workshop, seminar, convention, or conference.

The sad truth about these facts is that many employees don't like to attend workshops. One survey indicated that 70% of employees did not look forward to these learning sessions. These discouraging facts seem to indicate that businesses are spending big bucks to educate employees who don't want to attend these sessions.

The purpose of this chapter is to provide you with some basic principles that are needed to plan and implement a successful workshop, a workshop that employees are excited about attending. So, whether you're attending a workshop in the near future or you're responsible for organizing a session, this chapter will cover some valuable information that could make your job as an organizer or an attendee a lot easier. First, let's discuss the differences between workshops, seminars, conferences, and conventions. Then we'll cover nine steps to remember when attending or organizing a workshop.

WORKSHOPS, SEMINARS, CONFERENCES, AND CONVENTIONS

Many planners use the terms workshop, seminar, conference, and convention interchangeably. There have been workshops, seminars, and conferences with one speaker and 100 attendees. And there have been workshops, seminars, and conferences with hands-on instruction, 10 attendees, and no guest speaker. The point is that these terms have been so interconnected and mutually defined that most people don't know the differences among them.

While all four have an instructional mission, there are distinctions among them. In this chapter we will be using the following definitions of learning sessions:

Meeting: An assembly of people.
Workshop: Meeting for an exchange of ideas that also involves some hands-on experience.
Seminar: A meeting for an exchange of ideas. In college, it is a small group of advanced students involved in intense study under the guidance of a professor.
Conference: 1) A meeting for consultation or discussion. 2) A meeting to exchange information with a large group.
Convention: Formal meeting of members of a profession.

WORKSHOPS

Most businesses sponsor workshops where employees have an opportunity to get practical experience in order to improve their skills. Therefore, this chapter will focus on the basics of planning and conducting successful workshops. The information in this chapter can also be applied to coordinating seminars, conferences, and conventions.

Organizing a Workshop

The first and most important step in organizing a workshop is to determine whether, in fact, you need one. This may sound unnecessary to you, but you'd be surprised at the number of workshops that are scheduled that don't need to be. In fact, one of the reasons that workshops have such a negative image is because many are held when there would be a more successful method of instruction.

In some companies the same topic is covered in workshops every year. The employees are well versed on the subject; yet, they are gathered together to listen to the same information annually. This redundancy results in disgruntled employees who are wasting their time, while the business spends money that should be placed into a more beneficial educational program. Sound familiar?

In order to find out if your company really needs a workshop, ask the employees. Meet with supervisors to find out if customer relations is functioning well. Conduct a survey of administrative assistants to see if they fully understand sexual harassment. Look at the correspondence and attend public relations lectures at your business to find out if instruction in communication skills is necessary. And inquire about the type and degree of success of previous workshops at your business.

The bottom line is that you need to find out whether your employees really need to attend a workshop on a specific subject. Just because you or your supervisor thinks that a workshop on a particular topic is a great idea, doesn't mean that it's information your colleagues need.

You'll also need to determine whether your business can adequately handle a subject and if a workshop is the correct channel for instruction. For example, many computer workshops are held without enough hardware or staff to adequately handle the attendees. Sometimes workshops are scheduled when one-on-one instruction would be a better learning medium. Or many times a handbook would be a far better choice for understanding complex information. Ask yourself if your business has the adequate resources and if a workshop is the best choice of instruction for your material.

Second, you need to develop specific learning objectives for your workshop. If customer relations is your topic, then you must decide what you want your attendees to know as a result of the workshop. Workshop objectives could be written as follows:

Customer Relations Workshop—Objectives

1. To inform the attendees about the importance of creating a positive impression at work.

2. To inform attendees of the verbal and nonverbal communication necessary to conduct positive customer relations.

3. To motivate attendees to incorporate effective verbal and nonverbal communication into their interactions with customers.

Workshop objectives need to be written in such a way that you can evaluate their effectiveness. In the customer relations example, you can observe interactions and examine customer feedback to determine if your workshop has had an effect on customer relations. When you work with topics such as computers or writing abilities, you will have more quantifiable information to evaluate.

Third, it will be important to transform your workshop objectives into learning units with assigned times of instruction. If we break our customer relations objectives into learning units, we could arrive at the following structure for a one-day workshop. At this point, you can add in your break times.

Customer Relations—Learning Units for One Day Session

Registration and Coffee & Rolls	8:45–9:00
First Session—The Importance of Postive Impressions	9:00–10:15
Break	10:15–10:30
Second Session—Tips for Effective Verbal & Nonverbal Communication	10:30–11:45
Lunch	11:45–1:00
Third Session—Applying Powerful Telephone Skills	1:00–2:15
Break	2:15–2:30
Fourth Session—Successful Face to Face Interaction	2:30–3:45
Wrap-up	3:45-4:00

Fourth, you'll need to schedule the date, room, food, drinks, and audiovisual aids. After checking with the decision makers and your own calendar, schedule a day for your workshop. Most workshops are held toward the end of the work-week. The rationale is that most people are generally in a better mood toward the end of the week, so use agreeable dispositions to your advantage.

Some special events planners argue that Monday is the best day for workshops since people are generally more rested. In our experience, however, Mondays have been the day with the least-attended workshops. You may want to gather some input from your colleagues about the best day for scheduling a workshop.

As we discussed in Chapter 15, it's imperative that you check out the room for any type of meeting that you organize. You'll need to make sure that you have

REMINDERS FOR EFFECTIVE WORKSHOPS

1. Decide if you really need to sponsor a workshop on this topic.
2. Write objectives for your workshop.
3. Establish learning units.
4. Schedule the date, room, food, drinks, and audiovisual aids.
5. Select your session leaders.
6. Announce your workshop with an effective flier.
7. Prepare your workbooks, pens, handouts, and nametags.
8. Begin and end your sessions on time.
9. Ask attendees to fill out the evaluation forms.

enough chairs and table space for your attendees. Make sure that there isn't any external noise that could interfere with the speakers, and order refreshments for your group. Since you haven't spoken to your speakers yet, find out what type of audiovisual aid equipment you have access to.

Fifth, you probably already have some idea about who you want to lead the session for your workshops. Now's the time to contact these people and schedule them. If you are at a complete loss for who to contact, there are many fine training companies with excellent personnel that can instruct your employees.

Before you contact these session leaders, make sure you know how much money you can pay them, the length of their session, and what type of instruction you want them to use. It is always advisable to request some lecture and then hands-on training for your employees. So, in the Fourth Session on Face to Face Interaction, you could ask that a lecture/discussion period precede role playing and any other break-out sessions. Break-out sessions are times when pairs or smaller groups are given an interactive assignment based on the previous lecture, discussion, or readings.

It is also imperative that you ask your session leaders to prepare handouts for your attendees. Make sure that you can preview this material prior to the workshop, just in case you need to request any changes. Find out if any audiovisual aids are necessary and if the leader prefers a particular table or seat arrangement for attendees. As with any business deal, get your agreement in writing. Also ask for a short biography from the session leaders so that you or whoever is the master of ceremonies can make a proper introduction.

Sixth, as soon as you know the who, what, when, and where of the workshop, inform your attendees. It's always best to let people know as soon as possible, with

---

Looking for a Way to Make Your Job More Enjoyable?

✤ ✤ ✤

Interested in Tips for Getting Along with Difficult People?

✤ ✤ ✤

Ready To Receive the Positive Reinforcement You Deserve?

✤ ✤ ✤

We have the perfect workshop for you!
You'll learn how to create a positive impression
and get along effectively with just about anybody.

✤ ✤ ✤

JOIN US!

✤ ✤ ✤

WHAT: CUSTOMER RELATIONS WORKSHOP
WHEN: OCTOBER 7, 8:45–4:00
WHERE: SUITE 333
WHO: HUMAN RELATIONS STAFF
QUESTIONS? CONTACT BEV AT EXT. 33

---

two weeks being the minimum advance notification. Create an attractive flier to announce your workshop and always include the benefits to your employees. Try to make the workshop sound as interesting as possible.

Seventh, arrange to have notebooks, an outline of the day's activities, pens, nametags, and any handouts ready and available for the day of the workshop. Double check with your session leaders to make sure they have everything copied and ready to distribute.

Eighth, on the day of the workshop, have everything ready at least an hour before your start time. That way if you need to take care of any last minute changes, you'll have some time. Throughout the day, make sure that your sessions begin and end on time. And finally, at the end of each session or at the end of the day, have an evaluation sheet, like the one that follows, available for attendees to complete. You'll need to decide if you want feedback for each session or for the whole workshop. Generally it's best to create just one evaluation form. You'll usually get feedback on all of the sessions, and attendees prefer filling out only one form.

Following these nine simple steps will increase the effectiveness of your workshops.

CUSTOMER RELATIONS WORKSHOP EVALUATION FORM

How would you rate the ideas and content in this workshop?

5	4	3	2	1
EXCELLENT	GOOD	FAIR	POOR	UNSATISFACTORY

How effective was the presentation of material?

5	4	3	2	1
EXCELLENT	GOOD	FAIR	POOR	UNSATISFACTORY

Please rate this workshop.

5	4	3	2	1
EXCELLENT	GOOD	FAIR	POOR	UNSATISFACTORY

What did you most like about this workshop?

_____

_____

What did you least like about this workshop?

_____

_____

Special Considerations for Session Leaders

If you have been asked to lead a workshop session, the following six items should assist you in conducting an effective session.

First, if you're going to be paid to lead a workshop, get your contract in writing. That way there will be no dispute about when, where, and how much you'll be paid. Avoid the chance of any miscommunication by getting the specifics of your workshop in writing.

Second, be very clear about your learning objectives for your session as well as the overall objectives for the workshop. Having in mind your goals for yourself and the whole workshop will assist in creating your instruction.

If you're leading a session of 1½ hours, plan about 30 minutes of lecture and discussion, 45 minutes of hands-on experience, and the remaining time to wrap-up and review.

Third, always have a handout available. If you aren't covering any material that can be written on a handout, then provide the group with copies of stimulat-

REMINDERS FOR SESSION LEADERS

1. Get your contract in writing.
2. Be clear about your objectives as well as those for the workshop.
3. Plan a variety of instructional activities during your session.
4. Always have a handout.
5. Check out the audiovisual equipment prior to your session.
6. Get feedback from your participants.

ing and relevant articles that they can read at their leisure. People seem to think they're getting more if you give them a handout.

Fourth, make sure that your equipment works before your session begins. If you're having problems with the equipment, you can replace it or get assistance before the session begins. And always have an alternative plan just in case the audiovisual equipment doesn't work during your session. (It's a good idea to have an alternative option for almost everything that you plan.)

Finally, if the workshop organizer is not planning to evaluate your session individually, you may want to get some feedback from your participants. You could have a short evaluation form for them, or you could always ask them for some informal responses.

Speaking at a Workshop

Whether you are a leader or participant, there are several areas that you need to consider before you speak at a workshop. The following guidelines, in addition to the information in previous chapters, will assist you in delivering and facilitating dynamic presentations at workshops.

First, always be aware of your verbal and nonverbal delivery. As the leader of a workshop, you need to maintain a professional image, delivering both speeches and brief comments in an effective style. As a participant, you should be aware of your presentation at all times. A disheveled appearance or a question asked in an inaudible voice will not convey a professional image to colleagues, employees, or prospective clients who may be in attendance.

Second, always be clear about your speaking objectives. As the leader of a workshop session, you will need to communicate with the workshop coordinator so that you both understand the purpose and objectives of your talk. Always speak

---

REMINDERS FOR WORKSHOP SPEAKING

1. Always be aware of your verbal and nonverbal delivery.
2. Know why you are talking. Clearly convey your objectives to others.
3. Remember that interaction at a workshop is imperative. Focus on brevity, turn-taking, and an open exchange of ideas.

---

with the workshop coordinator about your plans for the session and if possible, share your handouts and audiovisual materials. It's far better to change your plans prior to your workshop than find out through participants' evaluations that you did not satisfy the advertised purpose of the session.

As a participant, you'll need to state what you have to say in a clear and coherent manner. Don't waste time by going off on a tangent when you ask a question or deliver a comment. Have a specific purpose for speaking and focus on being succinct.

Third, remember that a workshop should be an interactive environment for learning. While a workshop leader may lecture for a short period of time, the majority of the session should be spent on activities and a question and answer period. Neither the leader nor participants should dominate a session. By being clear and succinct, as well as polite, you will establish a productive exchange of ideas and turn-taking among participants.

By following these three simple speaking reminders at workshops, you will boost your speaking ability while increasing the productivity in your sessions.

Nice job reading the material in this chapter. Now finish this lesson by completing the following exercises and questions. Good luck!

EXERCISES

A. Prepare a hypothetical workshop. Select a topic that you and your colleagues need to have more information on. Organize the workshop as if your business was really planning to put it on. Create the most educational and interesting workshop that you can. After receiving feedback about the workshop from a few colleagues, show it to your supervisor. Perhaps your hypothetical workshop can become a reality.

B. Whenever you attend a workshop, analyze how it was structured. Examine the instructional methods, materials, and activities that were used. And always think about the strengths and weaknesses of the workshop. By analyzing other workshops, you will be able to apply what you learned.

Quiz

1. Explain the steps involved in organizing a successful workshop.
2. Discuss some reminders for being an effective session leader.

Answer Key

1. Some important considerations for organizing a workshop would include:
   a. Decide if you really need a workshop and if your business has adequate resources to conduct one.
   b. Define your learning objectives.
   c. Create your learning units and divide your information into timed sessions.
   d. Figure out the logistics (place, date, times, refreshments) of the workshop.
   e. Find your session leaders.
   f. Announce your workshop.
   g. Gather the materials.
   h. Make sure that everything runs smoothly and make sure that attendees evaluate the workshop.

2. If you are a workshop session leader you'll need to consider the following points:
   a. Get your contract in writing.
   b. Be clear about your objectives as well as those for the workshop.
   c. Plan diversity in your session.
   d. Always have a handout.
   e. Check out the audiovisual equipment.
   f. Get some feedback from your participants.

NEXT STEP

Another terrific job! Now, you're ready to move on to the next chapter, *Relating to All Cultures.*

CHAPTER | 18

RELATING TO
ALL CULTURES

As our global village becomes a reality, those of us in business recognize the necessity of understanding and respecting other cultures. Our global economy continues to grow stronger as more workers are traveling overseas, exportation continues to grow, and more and more immigrants are moving to the United States.

Consider these facts: U.S. investments abroad are estimated at $300 billion; 40 million tourists visit the United States every year; 10 million people immigrated to America in the 1980s. America is truly becoming an intercultural community.

In our competitive world, where marketing and communicating to people of diverse cultures can be translated into millions of dollars in sales, businesspeople need to be aware of and sensitive to cultures besides their own. Knowledge of intercultural communication involves appreciation and respect for other countries' languages, food, social taboos, and of course, verbal and nonverbal communication. The success of you and your business may depend on understanding and functioning with various ethnic groups.

This chapter will provide an overview of some cultural distinctions, guidelines for working with intercultural communication, and the problems with developing stereotypes. Let's begin with some areas in culture where differences are most likely to occur.

CULTURAL DIFFERENCES

When you examine the cultures of various countries, you will find differences in the use of language, gestures, space, and other aspects of communication. In some cultures, ignorance of foreign customs may not make a difference, but in other countries, lack of knowledge may result in a loss of business and good will.

In Japan, it is perfectly acceptable to drink a glass of *sake* with a business meal, whereas in Iraq or another Muslim country, ordering an alcoholic beverage may lose your account. If you were walking on the nude beach in Darwin, Australia, you might feel uncomfortable wearing clothes, while in Iran, women without a veil are scorned.

In Vietnam, offering your hand in friendship is considered in bad taste. And while in America, we have a few acceptable finger foods, in Africa, India, or Polynesia, you only eat with your fingers.

The point is that whether you do business in or outside of the U.S. with members of another culture, you need to be sensitive to their habits, customs, and taboos. Let's take a look at three areas of culture that may vary from group to group. We'll begin with a discussion of language.

Language

English is the primary language of more than 400 million people in the world. It is the most widely used language in the world and the most acceptable form for international business transactions. We should be aware of the differences that can and do occur in other languages, and be open to the fact that not everyone thinks or speaks as we do. Let's look at a few variations in language around the world.

First, we should recognize that a person's language not only provides a tool for relating to other people, but also is the means by which realities and perceptions of the world are formed. For example, in English we have one word for snow. When we want to be more specific in describing a certain type of snow, we use

WORDS FROM THE WISE

"The new electronic interdependence re-creates the world in the image of a global village."

—*Marshall McLuhan*

adjectives to describe white snow, dirty snow, firm snow, and powdery snow. Eskimos, on the other hand, have 25 different words that are used for snow. From an early age, Eskimos are taught to see the distinctions between types of snow. Their environment is different than ours, and English does not contain the variations that their language does. This phenomenon occurs frequently with other languages, and we need to be sensitive to its occurrence.

Second, there are cultures that do not place as much value on the spoken word as Americans do. Whereas many people in the United States believe that power lies in talking, Easterners place more emphasis on silence. It is not uncommon for a business executive in Japan to tire of a lengthy, and to them, unnecessary sales pitch. The person who speaks less is generally more popular and preferred.

Many Americans find long periods of silence between individuals disconcerting. They often jump to the conclusion that when there is a long silence, something is wrong. What we need to realize, however, is that other cultures view silence in a totally different light, and that our awkwardness is a result of the way we have been socialized.

Third, there are many words and phrases in English that cannot be translated literally into another language. For example, it has been reported that Pepsi created a marketing campaign in China based on the saying, "Come Alive." The Chinese translation turned out to be, "Pepsi Brings Your Ancestors Back From The Grave." The best-intentioned marketing promotions or public relations campaigns may just not work in another country.

Fourth, it's imperative to recognize that languages vary in respect to their use of certain phonetic sounds and accentuation. Thus, an inability of a person to pronounce English words correctly may not be a reflection on that person's intelligence but rather due to their country of origin.

Nonnative English speakers whose primary language is Spanish have been taught to speak differently than Americans have. For example, in English, one syllable of multisyllable words is accentuated, but in Spanish all syllables are pronounced almost equally. To incorporate accentuation is no easy task and can take

REMINDERS FOR USING LANGUAGE WITH OTHER CULTURES

1. Our perceptions of the world are shaped by language. Our language and our realities are not the only ones or the best.
2. Silence has varying degrees of value in other cultures.
3. Some ideas in English can't be translated literally into other languages.
4. Phonetic use varies from culture to culture. A brilliant Asian may have difficulty pronouncing some words in English.
5. Make sure the other person understands the meaning of a colloquial phrase.
6. Other cultures may use a nonassertive approach to language.
7. Make an attempt to learn some words in another language.
8. Speak slowly and distinctly, not louder.
9. Always use printed materials to explain and supplement your speech.

a long time for those of Spanish descent. In addition, the *th* sound doesn't exist so "they" becomes "day" and "that" becomes "dat" for Spanish speakers.

Spanish is the second most widely used language in America and there are predictions that by 2020, people of Hispanic heritage will be the largest ethnic population in America. Therefore, sensitivity to their language is important from both an economic and humanistic standpoint.

In some languages, articles like *a, an,* and *the* are not used, so "The boy has a cat" may become "Boy has cat." The bottom line is that in business, it is important to be sensitive to another culture's language and recognize that there are major differences in the way peoples of the world have been taught to communicate.

Fifth, not all colloquial sayings mean the same thing, even when they're spoken in English. Take for example, an unmarried American female who wanted a job with a major Christian broadcasting company in Australia. After her first interview went extremely well, she was invited out to eat with several of the top executives of the company. She almost ruined her chance for employment when she confessed, "You know I'm stuffed." Luckily for her, she was later questioned about her statement. As she found out, in Australia "I'm stuffed" means "I'm pregnant" and the company's strict moral code would have prohibited her employment.

"Throwing the baby out with the bath," "getting up on the wrong side of bed," and thousands of other colloquial phrases should be used only when you're sure the other person will understand their meaning. When using colloquial terms with people from other cultures, it's definitely better to be safe than sorry.

Sixth, people from different cultures may vary in their degree of assertiveness. The Japanese are so polite that in business they have a distaste for the word "no." As a result, many American businesspeople have interpreted such statements as, "We'll need to look into it further," "We're not sure," and "We'll do whatever is possible," to mean "yes," when in actuality the meaning was "no." Understanding a culture's intent and use of language can be most beneficial in business.

Seventh, try to learn at least a greeting and farewell in someone's native tongue. This is usually a fairly simple task and the other person will be complimented that you care.

Eighth, when another person is having difficulty understanding you, speak slower and more distinctly, not louder. When people are misunderstood, the natural reaction is to increase the volume. Avoid this tendency, as it could only make things worse.

Finally, always supplement your business speech or meeting with visual aids and other written materials. Your printed documents will clarify and explain your main points, avoiding any misunderstandings.

Gestures

Another area in intercultural communication that we need to be sensitive about is the use of gestures. When Russians clasp their hands above their head and shake them, as a boxer does in America to signify victory, their interpretation is that of friendship. When an index finger is tapped against one's temple in Europe, it means the other person is dumb. In America, the interpretation of the same finger against the same temple would be that the other person is smart. And while in America, the thumb and index finger joined to make a circle means "you're okay," in Italy, it's an obscene gesture. When people hitchhike in America, they extend their arm with their thumb up. If you exhibited that gesture in parts of Italy, you'd never be picked up, because the gesture is considered negative and derogatory.

Even gestures that you would think have shared international meaning, may not. People are generally surprised to find that shaking one's head up and down, which indicates "yes" in America, does not have that meaning in certain other countries. In Bulgaria and India, you'd need to shake your head from side to side—American's gesture for "no"—to indicate "yes." Things can get confusing!

The bottom line in using gestures from other cultures is to think about their use first. Some cultures use many gestures (Israel has over 275) and other cultures have fewer (America has approximately 70). The important thing is to be sensitive to another culture's nonverbal delivery. Watch other people, ask questions, and try to avoid using a gesture that will alienate anyone.

Space

Space is space, right? Wrong. All around the world, the amount of space a person needs varies. In the United States, people generally stand an arm's length away to have conversations with friends. Business transactions in a store or with a supervisor normally occur at a distance of between four and seven feet. An American's public distance—or the amount of space we like to keep between ourselves and noninteracting strangers—is beyond seven feet.

People from other cultures, however, may have a totally different perception of acceptable and nonacceptable space. In the Middle East, a salesperson may be breathing on you as he or she tries to make a deal. In extremely crowded countries like Japan and India, many Americans complain of feeling like a sardine in many business environments.

Appropriate touching also varies from culture to culture. Researchers categorize touching cultures into two groups: contact cultures and distant cultures. The contact cultures which generally touch more and require less personal space, include Latin American, Arab, Jewish, Eastern European, and Mediterranean. The more distant cultures include North American, Asian, and Northern European.

Thus, it's quite common to see heterosexual Italian men walking arm-in-arm down the street and Israelis kissing both cheeks of an acquaintance's face. Some Americans, Germans, and Asians may consider these behaviors only appropriate for more intimate relationships.

The important thing to remember is that appropriate space and touching seem to be relative, varying from culture to culture. And you should not judge a

REMINDERS FOR USE OF GESTURES AND SPACE

1. Recognize that cultures vary in terms of their use of gestures, space, and touching. It's your responsibility to find out the appropriateness of an act.
2. Avoid ethnocentrism at any cost. Our perceptions and behaviors are not necessarily the best.

group of people or a country based on one criterion alone. In business, as in life, it's best to have an open mind and learn from other people's behaviors.

SUBCULTURES

There are thousands of subcultures that exist in the United States today. A subculture is a group of people that is united by ethnic background, race, religion, social or economic status, or other characteristic. Many times a subculture will use a dialect where different pronunication, vocabulary, and grammar is applied to standard English.

Many people consider Black English to be the most distinctive social dialect in the United States. Black English is actually a combination of standard English and an African language and is recognized by such examples as loss of the *d* after a vowel ("food" becomes "foo") and double negatives ("I'm not going to feed you no more").

Many dialects are regional. You've probably recognized the difference between the way Midwesterners, Southerners, and New Yorkers talk. There are distinctive pronounciations and vocabulary for each dialect.

If you're doing a lot of business with people who speak with a dialect, it would be helpful for you to note the differences in their speech. And, in order to improve communication, make sure that you and your client speak distinctly and slowly, but not loudly.

STEREOTYPES

In this chapter we have discussed generalizations based on reality that can be made about various cultures. We have examined these organizational structures to heighten your awareness and to increase your ability to interact with people from other cultures. The end result should be a more positive relationship among cultures.

There are generalizations, however, that are not based on truth. Stereotypes are generalizations that are built on faulty perceptions and, as such, have no place in the business world. If you were to say that all Americans were brash and arrogant, you would be using a stereotype. Certainly, there are some Americans who are brash and arrogant, but we couldn't apply this generalization to everyone. There may also be many occasions when a particular individual does not fit the established generalization of his or her culture. There are Arabs who have a personal distance more than 10 feet or Vietnamese who are quite comfortable offering a handshake. The important thing is to be aware.

Stereotypes are derived from insufficient evidence and can be hurtful and nonproductive. It's important to make sure that your generalizations or those of your business are based on truth.

Now that you have finished reading the material in this chapter, it's time to work on the exercises and quiz. Take your time, do a great job, and good luck!

EXERCISES

A. Spend some time with a member of a culture different from your own. Did you observe any major differences in their use of language, gestures, or space? Did you notice any other interesting differences in their behavior? Can you apply what you learned to your interactions with all people from the same culture? Why or why not?

B. Learn at least a greeting and a farewell in another language. Use these words with someone from that culture. Note their reaction.

Quiz

1. Why should we become familiar with cultures outside our own?
2. What are some important things to remember about working with people of diverse cultures?

Answer Key

1. The world is becoming a global economic community where we are interdependent on many nations. The United States has $300 billion invested overseas, and immigrants are moving to America at a phenomenal pace. In order to create a positive environment for all cultures to work and grow, we must be aware and respectful of all people.
2. When we work with people of diverse cultures we must:
   a. Recognize that our perception is not the only or best one in the world.
   b. Be aware that the value of silence varies from culture to culture.
   c. Realize that the use of phonetic sounds varies from culture to culture.
   d. Try not to use colloquial sayings.
   e. Remember that other cultures are less assertive than Americans in their use of language.

f.   Learn some words in another language.

g.   Speak slower and more distinctly, not louder.

h.   Accompany a speech with written documents.

NEXT STEP

Way to go! You're ready to continue on to the next chapter, *Questions and Answers About Effective Communication.*

CHAPTER | 19

QUESTIONS AND ANSWERS ABOUT EFFECTIVE COMMUNICATION

There are always questions that need to be addressed before speakers give their presentations. This chapter is a compilation of the concerns of speakers who have had questions before they gave a presentation to an association, their departmental staff, or a group of potential clients. Read on and your questions may be answered, too.

QUESTION #1 After I have completed my public speech, what should I do? What if people have questions?

ANSWER #1 First, acknowledge your applause with "Thank you" or "I'm glad this topic is so important to you." Never look shocked or embarrassed that your audience liked what you had to say. You put in the time and effort, and this is your reward.

After the applause dies down, state that you will be answering questions. Let the audience know if you have a time limit before you accept questions. If the audience is in the dark, ask for the lights to be turned up. Ask anyone who asks a question to stand up and speak up. Always repeat the question after it is asked. By repeating the question, you will make sure that you understood it correctly and that your audience heard it.

Answer the question as succinctly as you can. If the question is one that has been answered in depth in your speech, say something like, "As I mentioned in more detail in my speech..." and then answer with an abridged version. If the question is one that you don't know the answer to, you could tell the person to meet with you after the session. At that point you could get his or her name and then follow up later.

If you are asked a question that you don't want to answer, use a connecting remark to take your audience to another area. You could say, "That is a solution that many people are examining today. I have another solution that would work. Let me tell you briefly about how I think the situation can be improved." Then you move on to a discussion about your solution. Answers like "No comment" or "That comment is inappropriate" may work when you're being investigated by a grand jury or when you're asked something very personal, but for most of your speaking engagements it will be better to use a connecting remark to take your audience to another place.

QUESTION #2   What should I do if I'm speaking in front of a group and there's a hostile member of the audience?

ANSWER #2   First of all, you need to realize that at some point in your business career you will encounter someone in the audience who thinks they have all the answers. If you ask yourself why this person isn't speaking to the group, you will probably conclude that you have more knowledge about the subject and few people want to listen to a hostile speaker. So, stay calm, turn your attention to positive members of the audience, recognize that, at least for this speech, you're the expert, and proceed with confidence.

If a hostile audience member begins heckling you, ask them politely to be quiet so that the other people may hear your speech or answer. If they continue to be obnoxious, ask them to leave. There is only one commander of your public speaking ship, and that is you! So take control.

QUESTION #3   I have to give a thirty-minute presentation to my department in three weeks and I don't know where to begin. What shall I do?

ANSWER #3   The first thing you need to do is to consider this experience in a positive light. Both you and your audience will learn something and the positive reinforcement you will receive will make the experience well worth the effort. Recognize that preparing your speech is a lot like working out. The benefits are tremendous but at first, it does seem hard to get started.

Jot down everything that you can think of that you'd like to say about the topic. Sit down at several different times and brainstorm. Converse with the people who will be at your meeting and find out what they're interested in hearing about. Do some research if you don't have enough information. Then start categorizing your material into three or four major points.

Third, use the three-part structure of introduction, body, and conclusion to organize your material. Write your body first by placing your main points into an outline. Connect your major points with transitions. Once you have the body together, look for an effective quotation, rhetorical question, or startling statistic to begin and conclude your speech.

When you're done writing your speech, rehearse it in front of friends, family, a videotape recorder, or a mirror. And remember, practice makes perfect.

QUESTION #4   My new job will be working in customer service. How can I excel at communicating with other people?

ANSWER #4   Keep a sheet by your desk that says "Customers want honesty, respect, and conciseness. A smile helps too." And then remember to incorporate these qualities into your own presentation.

A main part of working with the public is to listen. Look at the other person to see what they're saying with their words, the sounds of their voices, and their bodies. Try to figure out what they really mean when they say, "No one cares" at your business. In this popular period of automation and sterile interaction in business, you may provide the personal connection a person needs to continue doing business with your company.

As a result of effective listening, you will know exactly what your customer needs. Present your material in a concise and straightforward manner. If you don't have the answers, find out, and get back to your customer as soon as you can. Make sure that you always tell your customer what they need to know, not what you think they need.

QUESTION #5   My boss is always telling me to "hold my horses" when I start speaking at our staff meetings. I'm always the first person on the agenda. What can I do?

ANSWER #5   Whether you speak to a large audience or one person, there are several tips that will help you to gain control of the situation. Take a pause break before you begin to speak. Just count to two, look at the other person or people, smile if it's appropriate. Make sure to develop eye contact with someone, and then once you have your audience's attention, begin. Too many speakers rush into their presentation before people are ready to listen. Whether you're with one or three hundred people, make sure you have the attention of your audience before you begin talking. If you haven't engaged the audience before you've begun talking, don't count on them being with you throughout the presentation.

And on the same note, when you're finished speaking, pause, look at people and if appropriate, smile. Too many speakers will hide their head in their notes after their talk. Unfortunately, many people begin to wonder if the speaker is embarrassed or ashamed of their work. Practice a confident approach in both beginning and ending your presentations.

QUESTION #6   How do I know how much material I need for a thirty-minute presentation?

ANSWER #6   First, realize that the average person speaks approximately 130 words per minute. If you're writing an outline for your speech, you may want to approximate how many words you'll cover on each point. Most audiences will only be able to grasp a maximum of five main points over a thirty-minute period, so build your outline with this in mind. Also, if you're planning to use visual aids, your speaking time will be altered.

The only way to truly know how much material you need is to practice with what you have. When you've completed one-fourth of your outline, give your talk out loud. Then do the same thing when you've completed the next quarter and so on. Most professional speakers prepare twenty-five minutes of material for a thirty-minute speech. And somehow they always end up speaking for thirty minutes. Rehearsing your speech will not only determine how much material you need, but it will also help you build the confidence you need to do well.

QUESTION #7   I'll be delivering a speech at a national convention next month. I have been invited to attend a social function the night before my speech with most of the people who will make up my audience. Should I go?

ANSWER #7   Most definitely! By attending the social function, you'll have a clearer picture of who your audience is and what they need. You may learn something about the group that you didn't know before. Perhaps they are strongly against one of the proposals you are supporting in your speech or they already know all about your *StepOne Sales Project*.

You may also pick up some terms or examples that can be incorporated into your speech at the last minute. Or, you may learn some implicit information about the group that will fit beautifully into one of your main points.

Attend the function but spend most of your time listening. It will be your turn to talk the next day.

QUESTION #8   My supervisor has put me in charge of creating a speakers' bureau. What is it and where do I begin?

ANSWER #8   First of all, this is a great opportunity for you and your company to be recognized. A speakers' bureau is made up of a group of people from a business or nonprofit organization who go out into the community to speak on various topics. Some businesses prefer to have their employees speak on topics pertaining only to their business, while other companies are more flexible in respect to their topics.

Your first step would be to provide some information to employees about what you're planning to do. If your business has decided that speeches may be on a variety of topics, find out which employees have unique information on a particular topic. For example, if an employee is a member of an enviornmental group, then he or she may be able to talk about a nature topic. If someone has a hobby collecting Barbie dolls, he or she could talk about the changes in Barbies through the years. Or, if you have any employees with motivational life stories, you'll be able to find many groups who want to hear them.

If your business has decided that the focus of the speakers' bureau should be on your product then you can enlist help from people in various departments. Someone from the trust department could speak on investments, a loan officer could talk about starting a business, and a broker might address stocks and bonds.

Once you've decided on individuals' assignments, you can assist them in putting together a thirty- to forty-five minute speech. Make sure you include visual aids into each speech.

While your speakers' bureau team is rehearsing their material, you can get started on marketing the group. Prepare a promotional brochure and letter that explain who can speak and what topics will be addressed. Eventually you'll be able to send these materials to nonprofit organizations, libraries, and schools. You'll be amazed to find out how many groups want speakers (especially if the service is free). Follow up with a telephone call to the people who received your literature.

Keep track of where your employees go and follow up their talk with a call or survey to get some feedback. Make sure that any marketing materials, handouts, or other written materials have the name of your company, address, phone number, and logo on them.

The objective of your speakers' bureau is to spread goodwill throughout your community. Every speaker you send out should be well aware of your objective. This means that in addition to presenting a dynamic speech, they will be respectful, friendly, and courteous.

QUESTION #9   Last week I was presenting a controversial plan to my department. A colleague took issue with one point I was making. As she talked for five minutes, I shrank into my seat and didn't say a word. I hated my reaction, but I still don't know what I could have done. Can you help me?

ANSWER #9   First of all, let's examine this situation in a positive light. You've taken a critical step in learning by deciding you don't want to repeat a particular behavior again. Good for you! Now, the next time a situation like this occurs, you could deal with it in one of three ways.

If your critic is absolutely correct, admit it. Accept what she says calmly and move on to your next point. Be assertive and take over the discussion again. Think quickly and change the direction your discussion is headed. If the critic is right in blasting one item on your budget, agree with her and move on to other budget lines. Don't be overly apologetic or embarrassed. Everyone makes honest mistakes and you don't need to shrink on the vine because of it.

If you know that the criticism is based on emotion and not logic, empathize with your colleague and restate your main point again. A comment such as, "I understand what you're saying" can help. Try to neutralize an explosive situation. Your colleague may be mad at the way her day is going, the success you're having, or just plain mad. Don't take it personally. Rationality is the key.

If after restating your point several times, a colleague still doesn't understand what you're trying to say, suggest that you will be glad to meet with that person at another time so that the meeting can move along. Use a kind yet in control tone of voice and maintain eye contact with the critic.

QUESTION #10   In about one month I am going to be speaking to a group of over two hundred people. There will not be a podium and I don't know if I should stand in one place or move around. Any tips?

ANSWER #10   First of all, make sure that you have a microphone. Request a dual lavalier microphone that will attach to your clothing. A dual microphone has two microphones: one to use and the second as a backup in case the first microphone stops working. The lavalier will enable you to use your hands for gestures.

And to answer your question, you most certainly should move around. Don't be a frantic pacer but do emphasize major points with movement. Since you have a month to rehearse your speech, you can practice and include movement. Dependent on the arrangement of your audience, you can move forward or side to side. Just remember that you want your audience to remember your entire speech and not that you covered a lot of territory in front of them.

QUESTION #11   Every time I attend our staff meetings, one of my colleagues always talks about my ideas as if they were hers. Up until now I haven't said anything, but know I'm feeling that enough is enough. What action should I take?

ANSWER #11   There are three lines of action that you can take. First, you could stop sharing your ideas with her, then she won't be able to assume ownership of them.

If you must discuss your ideas with her prior to your meetings, you could talk with her about her behavior. Don't criticize her as a person, just tell her the specific times and words when she treated your ideas as her own. Maybe she's unaware of her behavior and you need to give her the benefit of the doubt.

If the previous two approaches don't work and she continues to use your material, then you'll need to be more assertive at your next meeting. After she completes stating your ideas, you could say, "Right, Beth. That is a good summary of my ideas about quality control, but I'm still working on the finishing touches on the plan. I'll have a completed proposal by next meeting." Or you could say, "Yes, Beth, that's almost the totality of my plan. But, I would like to add one central point to this idea that I've been working on for the last two weeks."

And of course, stay as calm and rational as you can when you make your statements. Everyone at the meeting will get the picture.

QUESTION #12   Our public relations department has planned a birthday party for our president. We expect over one hundred guests to attend and I've been asked to prepare a fifteen-minute recognition speech in our boss's honor. The party will be outside and now it's supposed to rain. We'll be under a ramada but the weather could get messy. How should I plan for this event?

ANSWER #12   Be flexible. You've prepared a fifteen-minute presentation, but be prepared to shorten it. Think about it. If the weather gets bad, who really wants to stand around and listen to any speech? Follow the lead of Hillary Rodham Clinton who in the spring of 1998 was scheduled to speak to the graduating law class of Howard University. When the weather turned bad and it rained heavily, she cut her speech by 11 pages. By the way, she was blessed by the crowd for her brevity.

QUESTION #13   Lately I've been reading about a trend in writing to use words with fewer syllables. Is this being advised in speaking?

ANSWER #13   There is one business organization that has recently advocated the use of words with two or fewer syllables instead of those with three or more syllables. An example they suggest is using words like *start* to replace *initiate*. Their objective is to expedite written correspondence in business. As of yet, we have not seen this same trend in oral communication in business.

QUESTION #14   Do you think anything will change in the area of public speaking?

ANSWER #14   The art of public speaking will always remain the same. The changes will occur in transmission of presentations. With the advent of state of the art video and computer mergers, we can expect easier and faster ways to send a presentation. For example, now many people are finding that CVideo Mail is an inexpensive and simple way to transmit both the verbal and nonverbal delivery of a presentation. CVideo Mail allows users to capture audio and video on their PC hard drive. Then users are able to send their audio and video message as an e-mail attachment. The software/hardware packages that you use to send CVideo Mail are becoming more affordable each year. The future will bring many more technological innovations that will impact public speaking.

QUESTION #15   What do I need to remember when I give a presentation?

ANSWER #15   Remember these three important rules whenever and wherever you speak:

1. Life is a learning experience and only through participation will we improve. The only way to succeed is to try.
2. The more you think about your subject and the less you think about yourself, the better you'll perform.
3. Be your best critic and reinforce yourself for any improvements you make.

NEXT STEP

Once again you've completed a chapter and are ready to move on. It's amazing what you can learn when you put your mind to it. Proceed on and continue your success!

CHAPTER 20

TIPS THAT TAKE YOU TO THE TOP

I t's true that we all learn from our mistakes. Sometimes, however, we could have avoided the hassle of making a mistake if only we had listened to someone's advice, or just received the advice in the first place. With this in mind, read through the following list of tips. Incorporate the material from this chapter into your modus operandi and maybe, just maybe, you can avoid making a mistake.

TIP #1   Always number your speech and meeting papers, handouts, reports, and any other written documents. You never know when you or someone else may drop your papers. By numbering your pages, your task of putting them in order will be a snap.

TIP #2   Keep a second copy of every presentation, handout, or other speech document you write. Either save your materials on a disk or have a written form in a file cabinet. Materials that seem useless today may become valuable in a couple of years. Become a pack rat when it comes to anything you write.

TIP #3   Always have a worthwhile handout with your presentation. You could make a copy of your budget or report, an article or a bibliography. The written documents will reinforce what you've said and increase your credibility. Handouts also demonstrate that you've spent some time on preparing your talk. Just make sure that all words are spelled correctly, your grammar is accurate, and you have one for everyone who attends the presentation. It's always better to have too many handouts than not enough.

TIP #4   If you're traveling to a conference or meeting, never, never pack with your luggage your speech, handouts, visual aids, or even the outfit you plan to wear on the day of your presentation. Carry all of these valuables with you. Luggage does get lost and stolen at airports and you certainly don't want your speech materials to drop down a black hole.

TIP #5   When you are writing your presentation, keep a sheet with the objective of your talk within sight. It will help you focus on what you should accomplish.

TIP #6   Keep all of your evidence current. There is nothing worse than using a 1980 census report as a basis for salaries or quoting a CEO who is deceased. Get in the habit of checking the dates on all of your sources.

TIP #7   A live demonstration or reenactment will be better than a lengthy explanation. Rather than spend 30 minutes explaining how to tune an engine, show the process. Or if some aspect of sexual harassment is your topic, recruit a couple of employees to act out potential problem situations, asking them beforehand for their cooperation, of course.

TIP #8   Always keep your presentation material simple and concise. Few people want you to ramble on in great detail discussing complex material. Leave the complexities for your handouts.

TIP #9   Try to arrive early to a lecture, meeting, or interview. You may get a chance to learn something from a colleague, and if you're presenting a talk, you'll have the opportunity to prepare the room and yourself.

TIP #10   When you're responsible for a meeting, speech, or other presentation, be prepared. Be ready with a concise definition for a difficult word in your report. Know how to change the bulb in your projector, and be able to turn down the air conditioning. Remember that you need to be able to wear many hats, and there's really only one person who's ultimately responsible—you.

TIP #11   When speaking at a meeting, conference, or workshop, always have a time limit for your material. Rehearse your presentation so you know exactly how long you'll take delivering your talk. Whether the time limit is self-imposed or decided by someone else, stick to it. Start on time and finish on time; your audience will thank you for it.

TIP #12   Always be on the lookout for material that you can use in your presentations. Clip and store articles, handouts, and other documents in your speech box or folder. You'll be glad you have them.

TIP #13   If you're responsible for scheduling workshop sessions, you should know that most people can sit and listen to a speaker for approximately one hour. After that, unless they are actively involved, they'll get antsy. Fifteen minutes is an adequate amount of time for a break between sessions. Before you break, synchronize watches in the room and write the returning time on the board or flip chart.

TIP #14   If you schedule a break sometime during your presentation, give the audience a reason to return. Give the audience an engaging preview of what you'll be discussing after the break. If you don't give them a reason to return, and unless they're being paid to be there, you may not see them again.

TIP #15   Try to schedule your business meetings in the morning. People are generally more productive then, and there's less chance that something else will come up during the day to interfere with the meeting.

TIP #16   Never rush during any type of presentation. Cut some of your material if you don't have enough time. There's nothing worse than hearing a speaker say, "I'll quickly go over these five points since I'm running out of time," and then because of a rapid delivery, no one in the audience absorbs any of the information.

TIP #17   When you have been asked to speak for 60 minutes, write a 55 minute speech. Inevitably, you will speak for 60 minutes.

TIP #18 When delivering your presentation, keep track of how long you've been speaking. Compare that time to how long it took to get to the same point during rehearsal. Then stay on track or cut some material so that you will finish on time.

TIP #19 If someone is going to introduce you to an audience, write out your own introduction. Include phonetic pronunciations and whatever else you want to be public information. This will eliminate having to make corrections later.

TIP #20 The most common criticism speakers receive is that they're not loud enough, they don't look at the audience, and they're boring. Prevent these comments by speaking loudly, looking at a variety of individuals in the audience, preparing interesting material, and being enthusiastic.

TIP #21 When you begin your speech, make sure that your audiovisual aid equipment is clean. Stopping in the middle of your talk to wipe off an overhead projector screen or erase a chalkboard is a waste of everyone's time.

TIP #22 If you must restate a point, repeat it in a different way. If someone doesn't understand your point the first way you stated it, saying it in the same way will not help the situation.

TIP #23 Never waste your audience's time with clerical tasks that you should take care of outside of the meeting. For example, never ask your sales force to sign their names on a sheet that's circulating when you have something very important to tell them. The signatures will just interfere with their comprehension of your material.

TIP #24 When in doubt about saying something, don't say anything. Wait until the boss approves your new proposal before discussing it at your business meeting. And never repeat secondhand information at a conference. Be patient; waiting until the appropriate time to discuss certain information is best for you and your business.

TIP #25 Facts and figures can be manipulated. When you read or hear some startling information, it's always a good idea to verify it with one or two other sources.

TIP #26   Remember that you are always communicating something to some-one. One cannot *not* communicate. If you're slouched over in your chair doodling on your pad during a business meeting, your boss may interpret this behavior as boredom. Or if you're always fiddling with your hair during a speech, people may spend more time watching your hair than listening to you. Unless you spend most of your time in solitary confinement, you will always be communicating.

TIP #27   As the popular adage states, "practice makes perfect." You can learn valuable information by reading hundreds of books on giving presentations, but unless you apply the information in your workplace, you won't improve your skills. So, volunteer to speak up and take every opportunity to improve your speaking abilities. Learn from your mistakes, be proud of the slightest improve-ments you make, and know that the most famous orators in history and the most successful CEOs have had to work at their abilities to speak in front of others.

TIP #28   The best way to improve your speaking abilities is through evaluation. Get in the habit of evaluating yourself and others. Keep a journal listing your pre-sentations with an evaluation of their strengths and weaknesses. Ask colleagues and your supervisor to evaluate your talks. Evaluate speakers on television and in person. And always remember that by recognizing and changing a mistake, you'll create a strength.

TIP #29   Recognize that by overcoming your fear of speaking in front of others, you have accomplished something that millions of people only wish they could do. By conquering the number one fear of Americans, you have proven to yourself that you can accomplish whatever you set your mind to. Speaking is both an art and a science and can be mastered by deciding that you will succeed. Have confi-dence in your ability to accomplish this important skill.

TIP #30   Recognize that you have your own unique style of speaking; thus, you should not be too hard on yourself when comparing yourself to other speakers. And get in the habit of positive self-talk about your abilities. Remember what Henry Ford once said, "Whether you think you can or can't, you're right."

NEXT STEP

Congratulations on completing our 20-step program to effective business speaking! You've worked hard to accomplish this task, and you should be commended for your efforts. Remember to use this text as a resource whenever you need some review about delivering business presentations. Continue your growth to becoming a great speaker!

ADDITIONAL RESOURCES

Carnegie, Dale. *How To Win Friends and Influence People*. New York: Pocket Books, 1975.

Cooper, Dr. Martin. *Change Your Voice, Change Your Life*. New York: Perennial Library, 1984.

Eakins, Barbara, and R. Gene Eakins. *Sex Differences in Human Communication*. Boston: Houghton Mifflin Co., 1978.

Eurich, Nell P. *Corporate Classrooms*. Princeton, New Jersey: Carnegie Foundation, 1985.

Fox, Grace. *Office Etiquette and Protocol: The Basics Made Easy*. LearningExpress, 1998.

Gelb, Michael J. *Present Yourself!* Rolling Hills Estates, California: Jalmar Press, 1988.

Hall, Edward T. *Beyond Culture*. New York: Doubleday & Co., 1976.

Hare, A. Paul. *Handbook of Small Group Research*. New York: Free Press, 1976.

Hoff, Ron. *I Can See You Naked*. New York: Andrews & McMeel, 1988.

Kanasik, Paul. *How To Make It Big in the Seminar Business*. New York: McGraw-Hill, 1992.

Knapp, Mark. *The Essentials of Nonverbal Communication*. New York: Holt, Rinehart & Winston, 1980.

Lakoff, Robin. *Language and Woman's Place*. New York: Harper Colophon Books, 1975.

Leeds, Dorothy. *Powerspeak*. New York: Prentice-Hall, 1988.

McManus, Judith, and Edward Osborn. *Creating an Effective Speech*. Denver, Colorado: Annie's Press, 1994.

Meyers, Judith N. *Practical Vocabulary: The Basics Made Easy*. New York: LearningExpress, 1998.

Monroe, Alan H. *Principles and Types of Speech*. New York: Scott, Foresman & Co., 1955.

Montapert, Alfred Armand, ed. *Distilled Wisdom*. Englewood, New Jersey: Prentice-Hall, 1964.

Olson, Judith F. *Grammar Essentials: The Basics Made Easy*. New York: LearningExpress, 1997.

Peters, Thomas J., and Robert H. Waterman, Jr. *In Search of Excellence: Lessons From America's Best-Run Companies*. New York: Harper & Row, 1982.

Prochnow, Herbert V., and Herbert V. Prochnow, Jr. *The Public Speaker's Treasure Chest*. New York: Harper & Row, 1964.

Seekings, David. *How To Organize Effective Conferences and Meetings*. London: Kogan Page Limited, 1992.

Simpson, James B. *Contemporary Quotations*. New York: Thomas Y. Crowell Co., 1964.

Slutsky, Jeff, and Michael Aun. *Toastmasters International Guide to Successful Speaking*. Chicago: Dearborn Financial Publishing, 1997.

Sorensen, Theodore C. *Kennedy*. New York: Harper & Row, 1965.

Sorrels, Bobbye D. *The Nonsexist Communicator*. East Elmhurst, New York: Communication Dynamics Press, 1978.

Strunk, William, and E. B. White. *Elements of Style*. New York: Macmillan, 1979.

Tannen, Deborah. *You Just Don't Understand*. New York: William Morrow and Co., 1990.

Valenti, Jack. *Speak Up With Confidence*. New York: William Morrow & Co., 1991.

Weil, Andrew, M.D. *Spontaneous Healing*. New York: Alfred A. Knopf, 1995.

Wood, Julia T. *Gendered Lives: Communication, Gender, and Culture*. Belmont, California: Wadsworth Publishing Co., 1994.

Zunin, Leonard, and Natalie Zunin. *Contact: The First Four Minutes*. New York: Ballantine Books, 1972.

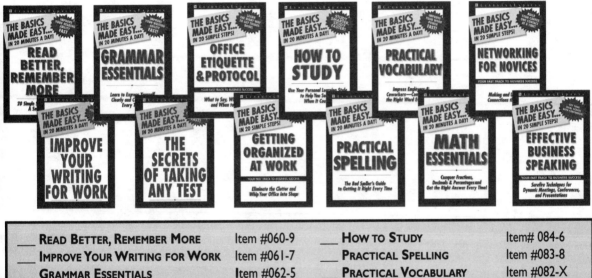
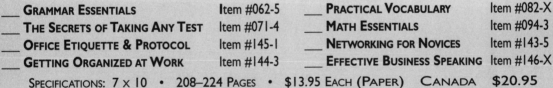

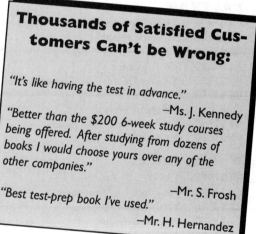

Order Form

CALIFORNIA EXAMS

- ___ @ $35.00   CA Allied Health
- ___ @ $35.00   CA Corrections Officer
- ___ @ $35.00   CA Firefighter
- ___ @ $20.00   CA Law Enforcement Career Guide
- ___ @ $35.00   CA Police Officer
- ___ @ $30.00   CA Postal Worker
- ___ @ $34.95   CA Real Estate Sales Exam
- ___ @ $35.00   CA State Police
- ___ @ $18.95   CBEST (California Basic Educational Skills Test)

NEW JERSEY EXAMS

- ___ @ $35.00   NJ Allied Health
- ___ @ $35.00   NJ Corrections Officer
- ___ @ $35.00   NJ Firefighter
- ___ @ $20.00   NJ Law Enforcement Career Guide
- ___ @ $35.00   NJ Police Officer
- ___ @ $30.00   NJ Postal Worker

TEXAS EXAMS

- ___ @ $18.95   TASP (Texas Academic Skills Program)
- ___ @ $32.50   TX Allied Health
- ___ @ $35.00   TX Corrections Officer
- ___ @ $35.00   TX Firefighter
- ___ @ $20.00   TX Law Enforcement Career Guide
- ___ @ $35.00   TX Police Officer
- ___ @ $30.00   TX Postal Worker
- ___ @ $29.95   TX Real Estate Sales Exam
- ___ @ $30.00   TX State Police

NEW YORK EXAMS

- ___ @ $15.95   CUNY Skills Assessment Test
- ___ @ $30.00   New York City Firefighter
- ___ @ $25.00   NYC Police Officer
- ___ @ $35.00   NY Allied Health
- ___ @ $35.00   NY Corrections Officer
- ___ @ $35.00   NY Firefighter
- ___ @ $20.00   NY Law Enforcement Career Guide
- ___ @ $30.00   NY Postal Worker
- ___ @ $35.00   NY State Police

MASSACHUSETTS EXAMS

- ___ @ $30.00   MA Allied Health
- ___ @ $30.00   MA Police Officer
- ___ @ $30.00   MA State Police Exam

ILLINOIS EXAMS

- ___ @ $25.00   Chicago Police Officer
- ___ @ $25.00   Illinois Allied Health

FLORIDA EXAMS

- ___ @ $32.50   FL Allied Health
- ___ @ $35.00   FL Corrections Officer
- ___ @ $20.00   FL Law Enforcement Career Guide
- ___ @ $35.00   FL Police Officer
- ___ @ $30.00   FL Postal Worker

REGIONAL EXAMS

- ___ @ $29.95   AMP Real Estate Sales Exam
- ___ @ $29.95   ASI Real Estate Sales Exam
- ___ @ $30.00   Midwest Police Officer Exam
- ___ @ $30.00   Midwest Firefighter Exam
- ___ @ $18.95   PPST (Praxis 1)
- ___ @ $29.95   PSI Real Estate Sales Exam
- ___ @ $25.00   The South Police Officer Exam
- ___ @ $25.00   The South Firefighter Exam

NATIONAL EDITIONS

- ___ @ $20.00   Allied Health Entrance Exams
- ___ @ $14.95   ASVAB (Armed Services Vocational Aptitude Battery): Complete Preparation Guide
- ___ @ $12.95   ASVAB Core Review
- ___ @ $19.95   Border Patrol Exam
- ___ @ $12.95   Bus Operator Exam
- ___ @ $14.95   Catholic High School Entrance Exams
- ___ @ $14.95   Federal Clerical Exam
- ___ @ $14.95   Pass the U.S. Citizenship Exam
- ___ @ $14.95   Police Officer Exam
- ___ @ $12.95   Postal Worker Exam
- ___ @ $12.95   Sanitation Worker Exam
- ___ @ $18.95   Treasury Enforcement Agent Exam

NATIONAL CERTIFICATION & LICENSING EXAMS

- ___ @ $20.00   Cosmetology Licensing Exam
- ___ @ $20.00   EMT-Basic Certification Exam
- ___ @ $20.00   Home Health Aide Certification Exam
- ___ @ $20.00   Nursing Assistant Certification Exam
- ___ @ $20.00   Paramedic Licensing Exam

CAREER STARTERS

- ___ @ $14.95   Administrative Assistant/Secretary
- ___ @ $14.00   Civil Service
- ___ @ $14.95   Computer Technician
- ___ @ $14.95   Cosmetology
- ___ @ $14.95   Culinary Arts
- ___ @ $14.95   EMT
- ___ @ $14.95   Firefighter
- ___ @ $14.95   Health Care
- ___ @ $14.95   Law Enforcement
- ___ @ $14.95   Paralegal
- ___ @ $14.95   Real Estate
- ___ @ $14.95   Retailing
- ___ @ $14.95   Teacher
- ___ @ $14.95   Webmaster

To Order, Call TOLL-FREE: 1-888-551-JOBS, Dept. A040

Or, mail this order form with your check or money order* to:

LearningExpress, Dept. A040, 20 Academy Street, Norwalk, CT 06850

Please allow at least 2-4 weeks for delivery. Prices subject to change without notice

*NY, CT, & MD residents add appropriate sales tax

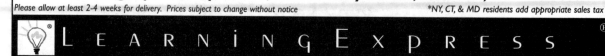